MACMILLAN MODERN DRAMATISTS

Macmillan Modern Dramatists

Series Editors: *Bruce King* and *Adele King*

Published titles

Further titles in preparation

MACMILLAN MODERN DRAMATISTS

GERMAN EXPRESSIONIST DRAMA

Ernst Toller and Georg Kaiser

Renate Benson
Associate Professor of German
University of Guelph, Canada

MACMILLAN PRESS
LONDON

First published 1984 by
THE MACMILLAN PRESS LTD
London and Basingstoke
Companies and representatives throughout the world

ISBN 0 333 30584 1 (hc)
ISBN 0 333 30586 8 (pb)

Typeset by
Wessex Typesetters Ltd
Frome, Somerset

Printed in Hong Kong

For Eugene

Contents

viii

List of Plates

1. Ernst Toller in 1927
2. Georg Kaiser in 1922
3. Toller's *Transfiguration* produced in 1919 by Karlheinz Martin and Robert Neppach at the Tribüne Theatre, Berlin
4. Kaiser's *From Morning to Midnight* produced by Viktor Barnowsky in 1921 in Berlin. *The snow field* sketch by César Klein
5. Kaiser's *Hell, Way, Earth* produced by Viktor Barnowsky at the Lessing Theatre, Berlin, in 1920. Sketch by César Klein
6. Mary Dietrich in Toller's *Masses and Man* produced by Jürgen Fehling at the Berlin Volksbühne in 1921
7. Profile of Erwin Piscator with model of the scaffold for Toller's *Hoppla! Such is Life*, first produced in 1927 in Berlin
8. Sketch by Otto Reigbert for Brecht's *Drums in the Night* produced by Otto Falckenburg in 1922
9. Paul Shelving's design of the English production of Kaiser's *Gas*, in 1923 at the Repertory Theatre, Birmingham

The author and publishers are grateful to the following for permission to reproduce plates: Akademie der Künste, Berlin, for Plates 1, 2, 3, 4, 6, 7, 8. Motley Books Ltd for Plate 5. The Mander and Mitchenson Collection for Plate 9.

Editors' Preface

The *Macmillan Modern Dramatists* is an international series of introductions to major and significant nineteenth- and twentieth-century dramatists, movements and new forms of drama in Europe, Great Britain, America and new nations such as Nigeria and Trinidad. Besides new studies of great and influential dramatists of the past, the series includes volumes on contemporary authors, recent trends in the theatre and on many dramatists, such as writers of farce, who have created theatre 'classics' while being neglected by literary criticism. The volumes in the series devoted to individual dramatists include a biography, a survey of the plays, and detailed analysis of the most significant plays, along with discussion, where relevant, of the political, social, historical and theatrical context. The authors of the volumes, who are involved with theatre as playwrights, directors, actors, teachers and critics, are concerned with the plays as theatre and discuss such matters as performance, character interpretation and staging, along with themes and contexts.

BRUCE KING
ADELE KING

Abbreviations and Conventions

For references to *Seven Plays by Ernst Toller*, E. Toller, H. Kesten and M. Baker Eddy (eds) (London: The Bodley Head, 1935), the abbreviation S.P. has been used. For references to *Ernst Toller, Gesammelte Werke/Kommentar und Materialien*, vols 1–6, John M. Spalek and W. Frühwald (eds) (Munich: Carl Hanser, 1978–79), the abbreviation T. plus volume and page number has been used. (The translations from this edition are my own.)

For references to *Five Plays, Georg Kaiser*, trans. B. J. Kenworthy, R. Last and J. M. Ritchie (London: Calder and Boyars, 1971) the abbreviation F.P. has been used. For references to *Georg Kaiser, Werke*, vols 1–6, W. Huder (ed.) (Frankfurt/M.: Propyläen Verlag, 1970–72), the abbreviation K. plus volume and page number has been used. (The translations from this edition are my own.)

1
Expressionism

They did not look.
They saw.
They did not photograph.
They had visions.[1]

While critics still are not certain when the term 'expression-ism' was first used, there is a general consensus that the movement known as Expressionism first manifested itself in Fine Art. A convenient date to mark the birth of Expressionism is 1905 for in that year a Paris exhibition brought together such painters as Matisse, Dufy, Derain and Rouault who were at once labelled *Les Fauves* ('The Wild Beasts') by the dismayed public and critics alike, because of the new and unconventional ways in which these artists used colour and form. In the same year in Dresden, Germany, a group of painters founded *Die Brücke* (The Bridge); among them were Kirchner, Schmidt-Rottluff and Heckel. These artists saw themselves, like the Fauvists, as enemies of conventional bourgeois art, and as prophets and creators of new values. They sought not mimesis but expression of a new vitalist feeling, the *élan vital*, and of their personal vision of the world. While Impressionism may be said to represent a subjective rendering of the visible world, Expressionism is basically the subjective expression of an inner world (vision); in representing his personal reality the artist has to free himself from all academic rules and traditional aesthetic concepts (especially traditional norms of beauty). The experience of the reality must be 'immediate' and 'genuine'; consequently the artist's *Ego* becomes a primary element in his work. While Expressionism manifested itself in many countries, it has come to be associated most closely with German art, literature, music (Schönberg), architecture (Gropius and the Bauhaus) and film (Wiene's *Das kabinett des Dr. Caligari*; Murnau's *Nosferatu*; Lang's *Metropolis*).

In 1911 *Die Brücke* moved to Berlin which by then had begun to supplant Paris as the capital of art. In their paintings the *Brücke* artists expressed ecstatically (through the use of bright, contrasting colours and new shapes) their vision of nature (animals, flowers, the sea) and the basic primitive joys of human nature associated especially with dance, music and eroticism. Their many religious paintings sprung from an inherent belief in the goodness of human nature, and the Christ figure became its ideal representative. But, as can be seen in Kirchner's *Strassen* ('Street Scenes'), 1913–23, they also reflected in their work a progressively sinister vision of a dehumanised and self-destructive world.

A second Expressionist group, *Der Blaue Reiter* ('The Blue Rider'), was founded in Munich in 1911 by Kandinsky, Marc, Macke, Klee and Jawlensky. Their aim was to revitalise art by tapping its primitive origins and in doing so they emphasised abstractionism (Kandinsky created his first abstract work in 1910); they also stressed the role of the artist as creator bound only by an inner imperative, and they insisted on the necessity of relating the arts to each other in a common synaesthesia. Kandinsky, who outlines these ideas in his influential treatise *Über das Geistige in der Kunst* (*On the Spiritual in Art*), 1912, was a close friend of Schönberg, and many of Kandinsky's paintings were called *Improvisation* or *Komposition* to draw attention to the fact that he wished to express musical dynamics through colours. Like *Die Brücke, Der Blaue Reiter* ceased to exist when the war broke out.

In German literature van Hoddis' 1910 poem 'Weltende' ('End of the World') is one of the earliest examples of Expressionism:

> The bourgeois' hat flies off his pointed head,
> the air re-echoes with a screaming sound.
> Tilers plunge from roofs and hit the ground,
> and seas are rising round the coasts (you read).
>
> The storm is here, crushed dams no longer hold,
> the savage seas come inland with a hop.
> The greater part of people have a cold.
> Off bridges everywhere the railroads drop.[2]

The poem combines two features of early literary Expressionism: its form is dominated by a series of seemingly unconnected and random images and, secondly, it is apocalyptic in its denunciation of the bourgeoisie and in its prophecy of imminent doom. Many of the new generation of German artists shared this apocalypticism which arose out of what Kandinsky called *Existentielle Angst* (Existential Fear); the world had become transparent, man was naked with nothing to cling to for support except his own *Ego*. The influence of Nietzsche, Schopenhauer, Darwin and Freud can be traced in nearly all these writers.

Heym's poems 'Umbra Vitae', 'Die Dämonen der Städte' ('The Demons of the Cities'), 'Morgue', 'Und die Hörner des Sommers verstummten' ('And the horns of the summer fell silent'), Werfel's 'Fremde sind wir auf Erden alle' ('We are all strangers on earth'), Trakl's 'De profundis', 'Ruh und Schweigen' ('Quiet and Silence'), Benn's 'Ikarus', Otten's story *Der Sturz aus dem Fenster* (*The Fall from the Window*) and many others reveal a clear vision of man's alienation and his existential fear. This feeling of imminent disaster was reinforced by the fact that the newly industrialised Germany was dominated by a military caste. Heym's 'Der Krieg' ('The War') and 'Der Gott der Stadt' ('The God of the City') are among the best examples of poems which speak prophetically of the outbreak of war and of a society corrupted by technology.

But despite their fears, these writers were also rebels who proclaimed ecstatically that a better society was to come. 'Aus Vision wird Mensch mündig' (Vision creates Man) wrote Kaiser, and it was this vision of a new world which dominated the first and 'ecstatic' phase of German literary Expressionism. Pinthus called his 1919 anthology of Expressionist poems *Menschheitsdämmerung* (*The Twilight of Humanity*) because the poets 'felt early how man was sinking into the twilight . . . sinking into the night of obliteration . . . but he would emerge again in the clearing dawn of a new day'. Their ecstatic *Schrei* (Scream) is for 'kindness, justice, comradeship, love of man for man . . .' because 'the world begins in man and God is discovered as a brother'.[3] *Aufbruch* (Departure) became the catch-word for the Expressionists' desire for transfiguration or moral regeneration. The names of many Expressionist journals similarly reflect this wish for a new beginning: *Der Sturm*, *Revolution*, *Die Aktion*, *Die weissen Blätter* (*The White Leaves*) and also Hiller's 1912 anthology, *Der Kondor* (*The Condor*). Typically, these writers, led by an overwhelming desire to destroy tradition, rejected the values of the previous generation. The generation conflict, especially between father and son, as depicted in Expressionist literature is unparalleled in German writing. Hasenclever's *Der Sohn*, 1914, Sorge's *Der Bettler* (*The Beggar*), 1912, and von Unruh's *Ein Geschlecht* (*A Family*), 1915–16, are prime examples of how the young writers viewed the father figure as a symbol of tyrannical authority and constraint; the murder of the father is a recurrent motif expressing symbolically their desire to liberate themselves from a stifling past. Wedekind explored this topic as early as 1891 in his *Frühling's Erwachen* (*Spring's Awakening*).

A major influence on the language of German Expressionism was exercised by the Futurist Marinetti who in an influential manifesto, *Technisches Manifest*, published in *Der Sturm* in 1912, laid down a number of rules designed to purify the language of bourgeois clichés. Marinetti argued that sentences should depend as far as possible on nouns and verbs and especially on the infinitive which conveyed a sense of the elasticity of experience; adjectives and adverbs were weak and should be avoided; analogies and images – especially those which were striking and unusual – should be used to relate nouns in a meaningful pattern; punctuation might be omitted and capital letters must be used much more extensively.[4] Stramm was so impressed by Marinetti's ideas on language that he destroyed his poems written between 1902 and 1913 and began again. His Expressionist writing, although slight – two cycles of poems, five short dramas (he died in the war in 1915) – is the most abstract of the early Expressionist phase. In his plays he no longer creates characters but types – Man, Woman – who express their feelings 'only in sound sequences within the rhythm of their actions'.[5] Language used this way comes to be known as *Telegrammstil* and may be illustrated by one of Stramm's poems:

Melancholy

Striding striving
living longs
shuddering standing
glances look for
dying grows
the coming
screams!
Deeply
we
dumb.[6]

Unlike Expressionist painters and composers – the latter influenced by Schönberg's *Harmonielehre* (*Theory of Harmony*) – Expressionist writers did not have a clearly defined programme. In fact many of the writers of the first phase did not associate themselves with Expressionism although they were agreed on common aims: the necessity to break with tradition, the need for a new language, the renewal of mankind. Furthermore, many of these writers had no chance to develop their art. Heym, Trakl, Stadler, Stramm, Lichtenstein – now considered among the greatest poets of Expressionism – were dead before 1920, most of them killed in the war.

The second stage of German Expressionism (1917–23) is associated primarily with drama, which is probably its most coherent genre. Its theme, the possibility of man's regeneration, is developed more fully than had been done

Expressionism

in Expressionist prose and poetry. Expressionist drama can be traced back to Wedekind (the *Lulu* dramas), Sternheim (*Die Hose*), and especially to Strindberg. His *To Damascus*, 1898, structurally and thematically anticipates many features of German Expressionist drama: the *Stationentechnik* (a non-traditional dramatic technique presenting the various stages of the protagonist's development), the transfiguration motif and the introduction of types instead of individual characters. Because this drama is based on autobiographical events it belongs to the category of the *Ich*, or *Bekenntnisdrama* (the I, or Confession drama). Sorge's *Der Bettler* follows Strindberg closely. The theme is the development of a youth (Sorge himself) into a man and his transfiguration into a better self; like Strindberg in *To Damascus* Sorge employs dream scenes in order to reflect inner experiences (the murder of the father, the death of the mother, a love-relationship with a woman whose child is from another man). Strindberg's Wanderer eventually leaves the world behind to enter a monastery; Sorge's protagonist, through his transfiguration, also turns into an outsider who in finding his *totales Ich* (the total I) feels released from all societal bonds and responsibility. The Wanderer and the Beggar are forerunners of *Der Neue Mensch* (the New Man), the ideal type of German Expressionist drama, especially that of Ernst Toller and Georg Kaiser.

Because German Expressionist drama was different in its conception of man and in the language with which it treated its themes, it also evolved a distinctive Expressionist style of performance which one critic has subdivided into three general styles: (1) the *Geist* (Spirit) *performance*; (2) the *Schrei* (scream or ecstatic) *performance*; (3) the *Ich performance*. The *Geist performance*, the most abstract, may be seen 'as an ultimate vision of pure expression

7

without the conventional intervention of dramatic characters or intricate plot'. Stramm's plays were most suited for
this kind of performance. The *Schrei performance* can be
compared 'to an actual, if hazy, intense dream-state, where
movement, exteriors, language, motivation, and inner logic
were uniformly and bizarrely warped'. The *Ich performance* resembles the *Schrei performance* but differed in
that it focused upon a central character.[7] Performances of
Toller's *Die Wandlung* (*Transfiguration*) and *Masse
Mensch* (*Masses and Man*) demonstrated these two styles
most purely. Actors often used exaggerated gestures,
masks, or mask-like make-up, to portray human types, and
'ecstatic' or dynamic speech to convey a renewed or
'extraordinary' state of being.

New stage techniques were also developed for Expressionist drama. The main influence came from Appia and
Craig whose theoretical works *La musique et la mise en
scène* (1899) and *The Art of the Theatre* (1905) were
immediately published in German. Both advocated abstract stage design with emphasis on geometrical forms and
'dramatic' lighting. In a 1913 production of part of Gluck's
Orpheus und Euridike at Hellerau, Appia designed the set
which 'consisted solely of steps, ramps, platform and
directional lighting'.[8] The dance sequences choreographed
by Jacques-Dalcroze anticipated the stylised movement
which was to become an integral part of German Expressionist staging, especially in crowd scenes. Germany's
most famous director, Max Reinhardt, used directional
lighting in his 1917 production of Sorge's *Der Bettler*.
Another influence came from Antoine's *Théâtre Libre* and
the German *Stilbühne* which stressed simplicity in staging
and dispensed as much as possible with props. But it was
the younger generation – some of them pupils of Reinhardt
– who fully developed Expressionist stage techniques. The

most noteworthy among them were Falckenberg, Hellmer, Fehling, Martin and Leopold Jessner. Jessner became famous for the use he made of Appia's steps; they became known as *Jessnertreppen* – a 'single flight of steps raked back from the front of the stage' (as in his 1920 production of *Richard III*). But they were more than just steps, writes a contemporary, Kenneth Macgowan: 'Jessner fills his stage with steps. He seems unable to get along without them. He must have platforms, levels, walls, terraces. They are to him what screens, towering shapes, great curtains are to Gordon Craig'.[8]

When the Nazis came to power in 1933 they regarded Expressionism as degenerate and set about destroying all evidence of it (no prompt book for any major Expressionist drama production exists). It is a tragic irony, as Pinthus notes, that young German audiences after 1945 only became acquainted with Expressionism through the works of foreign writers like T. S. Eliot, Eugene O'Neill, Thornton Wilder and Tennessee Williams who themselves had been influenced so powerfully by German Expressionists.[10] In the field of drama the most important influence was exercised by Ernst Toller and Georg Kaiser; their work is central to the development of Expressionism on stage.

2
Ernst Toller: Art and Politics

'A Jewish mother bore me, Germany nursed me, Europe educated me, the earth is my homeland, the world my fatherland.' (T. 4/228)

Although Ernst Toller achieved international fame as a dramatist in the 1920s – his plays were translated into more than twenty languages – his work and reputation have suffered a severe decline that derives, in part, from peculiar historical and political factors. Because he was Jewish, and because he was an outspoken opponent of Nazism, his writings were proscribed in 1933 and the staging of his plays in Germany forbidden. Following the end of the Second World War, when it might have seemed his reputation would be rehabilitated, he fell victim to the Cold War and the West's distrust of Communism. West Germany, in the 1950s and 1960s, had little liking for the 'red' Toller; in 1977 only one of Toller's plays, *Hoppla, wir leben*! (*Hoppla! Such is Life!*) was in print there. Since 1978, thanks to the work of the scholars W. Frühwald and

10

J. M. Spalek, Toller's work is available again and a fresh appreciation of his art is now possible.

Ernst Toller is an important writer because of his association with German Expressionism, the first genuine artistic movement in twentieth-century Germany. He is important also because his work, unlike that of the mainstream of German writers, is intensely political. Like Lessing, Büchner and Heine before him, he is an *engagé* writer, mirroring the tensions of troubled post-First World War Germany and anticipating the cultural and moral anarchy of twentieth-century Europe which was to lead to the fascism of Mussolini's Italy, the Nazism of Hitler's Germany and the totalitarianism of Stalin's Russia.

Toller was born in 1893 in the small German town of Samotschin on the border of West Prussia. His father was a prosperous merchant and a town councillor. His mother's grandfather had been the first Jew allowed to settle in Samotschin. In his autobiography, *Eine Jugend in Deutschland* (*I Was a German*), 1933, Toller notes that in the bourgeois outpost that was Samotschin the Jews made their homes centres of German literature, philosophy and art. Indeed they usually joined forces with the Germans in street fights with the Poles. He expresses his dislike of the rigid class system which promoted intolerance and rivalry between nationalities. He also expresses his awareness of the anti-semitism that was a part of German and European thought. In Samotschin he developed a lifelong sympathy for the underprivileged who would become the protagonists of a number of his dramas.

When he became a student at high school in the nearby town of Bromberg, he wrote a column for the local paper, the *Ostdeutsche Rundschau*. Especially memorable – and typical – is his account of the death of a poor half-wit of Samotschin who died of an epileptic attack:

11

> Last week, the worker Julius died. He was lying at the Railway Station from 3 a.m. until 9 a.m. suffering from convulsions without anyone helping him or calling a doctor. How could it happen that young street urchins could throw stones and water at a dying man? When the police were notified they claimed that it was none of their business because Julius was lying on the property of the Royal Prussian Railways. How could they cling to the letter of the law when the life of a human being was at stake? (T. 4/30–1)

The sentiments of this early passage anticipate Toller's lifelong concern for the individual and his deep-seated distrust of institutions which he perceived as heartless and inhuman. Julius became, in part, the model for the characters of the mad cripple in *Die Wandlung* (*Transfiguration*); he can be traced also in the Old Reaper in *Die Maschinenstürmer* (*The Machine-Wreckers*), Pickel in *Hoppla, wir leben!* and Pipermann in *Pastor Hall*.

After he finished high school Toller spent six months – from February to July of 1914 – studying law at the University of Grenoble, France. He did not know yet what he wanted to become and he read randomly in the writings of Kant, Nietzsche, Dostoevski and Tolstoy. His private reading during high school had included Hauptmann, Ibsen, Strindberg, Wedekind – modern dramatists whom his teachers despised.

On the outbreak of the First World War young men everywhere in Europe were fired with a patriotic zeal to fight for King and Country. Toller has recorded the almost mystical fervour with which he too welcomed war:

> Yes, we are living in a state of emotional frenzy. Words like Germany, Fatherland, War have a magic power

when we pronounce them; they do not vanish, they float in the air, they circle around themselves, they inflame themselves and us. (T. 4/53)

Like many German Jews, Toller was anxious to demonstrate his patriotism, and he enlisted immediately in the Artillery. His first six months were spent near Strasburg until, tiring of the routine, he asked to be transferred to the front. He was sent to Verdun in March 1915 and he fought through the savage battles that took place there between February and May of 1916. A particularly traumatic event triggered his rejection of war. He was digging a trench when he realised that his pickaxe had become stuck in the entrails of a man who had been buried there:

And, suddenly, as when darkness parts from light, the word from the idea, I grasp the simple truth about mankind which I had forgotten, which had been buried in me. Communion, unity and the principle which unites mankind. A dead man. Not a dead Frenchman. Not a dead German. A dead man. (T. 4/70)

It is this concern for the individual which prevented Toller from ever embracing completely the collectivism of any system, even that of Marxism to which he was sympathetic. As one critic puts it, 'He did not want *Masse*, he wanted Mensch'.

In January 1917 Toller, suffering from a heart ailment and probably from a nervous breakdown, was put on the inactive list. For a time he led an uneventful life as a student at the Universities of Munich and Heidelberg, studying literature and sociology. At Munich he met many of Germany's leading writers including Frank Wedekind, Rainer Maria Rilke and Thomas Mann, who read his early

13

work and encouraged him to be a writer. At Heidelberg he studied with the sociologist Max Weber and he founded a pacifist group of students. When the group was ruthlessly suppressed by the military he fled to Berlin, where he met Kurt Eisner, the pacifist leader of the Independent Social Democratic Party in Munich (USPD), a splinter group of the Social Democratic Party. Its aim was the liberation of the proletariat who would in future govern themselves within a classless society in a community of nations united in brotherhood. Toller was already profoundly influenced by the writings of Gustav Landauer – especially by his *Aufruf zum Sozialismus* (*Call for Socialism*) – and had been corresponding with him since late 1917. Toller followed Eisner back to Munich where both were arrested because of their involvement in the strike of munition workers. Toller spent three months in prison, where he busied himself reading the works of Marx, Engels, Lassalle, Mehring and Bakunin, among others. 'Only now', writes Toller in his autobiography, 'did I become a socialist. My eyes are being opened to see the social structure of society, the limitations of warfare and the terrible falsity of the law which allows everybody to starve but only a few to get rich; I begin to understand the interrelations between capital and work and realise the historical significance of the working class' (T. 4/95). His first play *Die Wandlung*, which he finished in March 1918, clearly reflects his newly-won perspectives. After his release from prison he spent four days under psychiatric observation by the well-known and eccentric Professor Kräpelin who had formed a league for the overthrow of England. Kräpelin became the model for the psychiatrist Lüdin in *Hoppla, wir leben*!

With the collapse of the second German Empire in November 1918, the Provisional Government, led by the

Social Democrats, was threatened by forces on the extreme Right and Left. The Left sought to bring about social change on a Communist pattern and the Right wanted to continue the monarchic course. Worker's and Soldier's soviets sprang up all over Germany. In Munich, Kurt Eisner formed a provisional soviet-style Bavarian Government in November 1918 and Toller was elected Vice-President of the Central Committee of Workers', Farmers' and Soldiers' Council. When the Republic was finally crushed on 30 April, many of Toller's friends and acquaintances were summarily executed. (Both Kurt Eisner and Gustav Landauer were savagely murdered.) Toller, who had gone into hiding, was eventually denounced and in July 1919 was sentenced to five years imprisonment.

The premiere of his play, *Die Wandlung*, on 30 September 1919, made Toller famous overnight and it led the Bavarian Minister of Justice to offer him a pardon after only six months in prison. Toller rejected the offer on the grounds that he wanted *justice* for himself and his fellow prisoners, not a pardon. His writings while in jail represent an impressive contribution to prison literature. With astonishing energy he created four full-length plays: *Masse Mensch* (*Masses and Man*), premiered in 1920; *Die Maschinenstürmer*, premiered in 1922; *Hinkemann*, probably his best play, first staged in 1923; *Der entfesselte Wotan* (*Wotan Unbound*), a satire on Hitler, written and published in 1923 and first produced in a Russian translation in 1924 at the Moscow Bolshoi Dramatic Theatre, directed by K. P. Chochlow. He also wrote a puppet play, *Die Rache des verhöhnten Liebhabers* (*The Scorned Lover's Revenge*), 1920; three cycles of poems: *Gedichte der Gefangenen* (*Prisoners' Poems*), 1921; *Vormorgen* (*Before Dawn*), 1924; *Das Schwalbenbuch* (*The Swallow Book*), 1924. He wrote a choral work, *Der Tag des Proletariats* (*The Day of the Proletariat*), 1921, and a scenario, *Bilder aus der grossen französischen Revolution* (*Pictures from the French Revolution*), 1922.

Das Schwalbenbuch, which contains some of his most beautiful poems, grew out of two incidents that symbolised the prisoners' plight. In one of those incidents a young pair of swallows began nesting and raising their young in Toller's cell. Toller was enchanted by their company and the swallows became the focal point of a number of poems expressing his hopes and fears.

> You are like the poet, my swallows.
>
> Although men cause them suffering, they love
> mankind with never ending ardour,
> they who are so much more akin to the stars,
> to the stones, to the tempest, than to any
> human being.
>
> You are like the poet, my swallows.
>
> (T. 2/329)

In 1927 Toller published *Justiz. Erlebnisse* (*Experiences with Justice*) which depicts in chilling detail the injustices of the Bavarian judicial and penal system. There is no doubt that he suffered severely from his imprisonment: his letters speak of recurrent headaches and insomnia, he shows an increasing irritability, he is plagued by thoughts of suicide, he expresses a deep pessimism about Germany's political future. What sustained him in his most despairing periods was his deep-felt belief in the ultimate moral regeneration of mankind and the possibility of a new and better social order. In his autobiography he writes:

No, I was never alone in these five years, never alone

even in the most desolate solitude. The sun, the moon,
and the wind gave me comfort . . . the grass growing in
the spring between the stones of the courtyard gave me
comfort as did a friendly glance, a greeting from beloved
people, and the friendship of my comrades. And I drew
comfort from my faith in a world of justice, freedom,
human kindness, in a world without fear or hunger.

(T. 4/235)

After his release from prison in 1924, Toller combined
intense political activity and travel with writing. In 1925 he
visited the Near East, Palestine and England; in 1926 he
travelled to the Soviet Union explaining and defending his
role in the Munich Revolution. In 1927 he visited Austria
(to attend performances of *Hinkemann* and *Masse Mensch*
in Vienna), Belgium (where he became firm friends with
Jawaharlal Nehru), Denmark (where he delivered a eulogy
on the occasion of the death of the critic Georg Brandes),
and Norway. In 1929 he travelled to the United States and
Mexico and lived in Spain for periods in 1931 and 1932.
His political activities included organising help for the
political prisoners Max Hölz and the Communist Expressionist writer J. R. Becher; he also joined the 'Gruppe
revolutionärer Pazifisten' ('Group of Revolutionary
Pacifists') whose members included Kurt Hiller, Walter
Mehring and Kurt Tucholsky.

During these years Toller produced five plays: *Hoppla,
wir leben*!, 1927; *Bourgeois bleibt Bourgeois* (an adapta-
tion of Molière's *Le Bourgeois gentilhomme*, co-authored
with Walter Hasenclever and Hermann Kesten), 1929;
Feuer aus den Kesseln (*Draw the Fires*), 1930; *Wunder in
Amerika* (*Miracle in America*, co-authored with Herman
Kesten), 1931; and *Die blinde Göttin* (*The Blind Goddess*),
1932. His radio play, *Berlin, letzte Ausgabe* (*Berlin, Last*

Edition), 1928–29, has not yet been published. In these plays, Toller remains as political as ever; however, his social utopianism, his belief in the possibility of a humane brotherhood of men, has been somewhat tempered by practical experience; he was especially concerned about the growth of Hitler's party. His play *Der entfesselte Wotan* already depicts Hitler in 1923 as a ruthless megalomaniac. On New Year's Eve, 1931, Toller wrote prophetically about Hitler's assumption of power:

> It is said that people don't learn from the past; apparently they don't learn from the present either. Otherwise they would remember what methods were used by Mussolini, Pilsudski and others. Chancellor Hitler, with one stroke of his pen, will get rid of the achievements of Social Democracy on which the party prides itself so much. Overnight all Republican and Socialist government officials, judges, police officers will be removed and replaced by reliable fascist cadres.
>
> (T. 1/71)

In January 1933, Hitler came to power and on 28 February he issued a 'Bill for the Protection of the People and the State' which suspended the guarantee of personal liberty granted under the Weimar Republic. It was fortunate that Toller was in Switzerland for many of his friends, including Carl von Ossietzky, Erich Mühsam and Kurt Hiller, were arrested. When Toller's books were burned on 10 May 1933, he wrote an open letter to Josef Goebbels, Minister of Propaganda, who was responsible for this infamous act: 'You pretend to save German culture, but you destroy its most noble products. You pretend to awaken German youth, but you blind their minds, their eyes and senses. You pretend to purify Germany of its criminals, but you prosecute the weakest people, the Jews' (T. 1/77). In August Toller, along with thirty-three other Germans who included Alfred Kerr, Heinrich Mann, Kurt Tuckolsky and Leon Feuchtwanger, was stripped of his German citizenship.

In the years of exile that followed – from 1933 until his death in 1939 – Toller continued his political activities and his writing. Several of his plays were performed in England, *The Blind Goddess* in 1934, and *Draw the Fires* in 1935. In 1936 his comedy, *No More Peace* (*Nie wieder Friede!*),[1] translated by Edward Crankshaw, with lyrics adapted by W. H. Auden and music by Murill, had its premiere at the Gate Theatre, London, with the young German actress Christiane Grautoff in the leading female role. She had followed Toller into exile and they were married in May 1935. A number of his writings were published in England by the Bodley Head Press; Sean O'Casey, the famous Irish playwright, reviewed them enthusiastically:

Of the seven plays, *Masses and Man* and *The Machine Wreckers* are the best, I think, but each has something to say, and all have in them that fierce outcry against the world's woe that is the strongest and shrillest note in every song that Toller has to sing. Here are plays for the modern theatre whether one likes them or not; whether they glorify one's pant [*sic*] for politics, or whether they provoke one to a hasty and hot condemnation of their implication. Each play is a serious reflection from a worthy and intelligent dramatist. (T. 6/206)

In 1936 he went to the United States and Canada on an extended lecture tour and was engaged as a scriptwriter by Metro-Goldwyn-Mayer, joining other emigré writers like Franz Werfel and Carl Zuckmayer. (In 1931 Toller had collaborated with Walter Hasenclever on the German version of the MGM 1930 film, *The Big House*, *Menschen hinter Gittern*.) But Toller's scripts, 'Lola Montez' and 'The Way to India', were never used. In 1938, he let his MGM contract lapse; the transition from German to English proved too difficult for him as it did for most of the German emigré writers. For example, Toller's last play, *Pastor Hall*, was rejected by Barret H. Clark, Executive Director of the Dramatists Play Service (and a good friend of Toller). His reasons illustrate the difficulties so many European writers faced in America:

> Specifically, I speak of the language of the translation. Well, it is here and there satisfying and it no doubt is English, but English is no longer *our* language here. I began to mark a word or a sentence here and there, and then I quit. The *music*, the rhythm, are so consciously English that a good part of the time I feel I am reading a more or less dead language. There is very little colour in it and none (or almost none) of that lyric quality which I find in the original German of your other work.
>
> (T. 6/218)

The rejection of the play was one of a number of setbacks suffered by Toller at this time. His health began to deteriorate in 1937 and he was plagued by severe head-aches and insomnia. In 1938 his marriage was dissolved, and for the first time in his life he experienced financial hardship. However, Toller continued to write and give lectures and he took up yet another political cause. He started a Spanish Help Action, working tirelessly seeking international aid for the victims of the Spanish Civil War. He enlisted the help of the world press and such interna-tional figures as Picasso, H. G. Wells and Thomas Mann, and he was eventually successful in persuading President Roosevelt to establish a Committee to raise fifty million dollars for the Spanish population. However, in March 1939 Franco's troops crushed the last of the Republican opposition and on 1 April recognition of Franco's regime by France, Britain and the US brought Toller's Help Action to an end. On 22 May, Toller hanged himself in the Hotel Mayflower in New York.

For Toller, who had spent all his life opposing fascism, the action of the democracies must have seemed a profound betrayal of all he believed in and an omen of their inability to defend themselves against the most destructive of the fascist ideologies – Nazism. Frühwald suggests that his suicide was a final individual gesture of revolt desperately reaffirming his opposition to Hitler. Toller's last message, 'The Last Testament of Ernst Toller', is a call to the democracies to rally in defence of freedom; it is a noble restatement of all he had attempted in his life and work:

> The threatened culture can be saved only if the subjugated nations keep alert the desire for freedom, justice, and human dignity and if this desire becomes so elementary that the desire turns into will and will into action.
>
> (T. 1/270)

3
The New Man: Birth and Crucifixion

'Die Wandlung' ('Transfiguration')

Die Wandlung was written in the midst of a war. I mimeographed the scenes in the military hospital and handed them out to women during the strike at the beginning of 1918. I had then only one thing in mind while writing: to work for peace. (T. 1/137)

Die Wandlung, Toller's first drama, begun in 1917 and finished in March 1918, is a *Stationendrama* which in every aspect (composition, content, structure and language) established Toller at once as a major Expressionist dramatist beside Kaiser, Sorge and Hasenclever. It dramatises the various stages of a young man's transformation from immaturity to maturity, from a deep sense of human estrangement to a mystical sense of mankind's future redemption. The protagonist comes to an understanding of the horrors and futility of war and finally espouses a vision of the brotherhood of all humanity, liberated from poverty and political oppression. Because of its autobiographical aspects, in essence Toller's war experiences between 1914 and 1917, it can be called a *Bekenntnisdrama* (confession drama); because of its ecstatically proclaimed ideology of human brotherhood, it is also an *O Mensch-Drama*.

In *Die Wandlung* Toller employs and pushes to the extreme the form of the *Stationendrama*, a form already used by Strindberg in *To Damascus* (1898) and further developed by Kaiser in *Von morgens bis mitternachts* (*From Morning to Midnight*), 1912. This particular dramatic form allows Toller to escape the rigidity of the traditional form of drama with its exposition and development through climax to the catastrophe or denouement. Place and time in *Die Wandlung* are indicated only in the most general manner in order to convey a sense of the universal and the timeless: it is 'night' or 'evening' or 'morning'; the action of the play takes place 'in Europe before the beginning of rebirth'. The *dramatis personae* are types, symbolic figures of humanity. Only two of them have proper names: Friedrich, the protagonist (the name has obvious associations with *Frieden*, German for 'peace'), and Gabriele, the woman he loves.

Die Wandlung is organised in six 'stages' ('stages' in a technical sense of dramatic movements and 'stages' in the sense of varying moments of human development) which are further divided into thirteen tableaux. Toller, like Strindberg and Kaiser who may have influenced him in this regard, constructs his play almost mathematically. The thirteen tableaux of *Die Wandlung* are built around the climactic seventh tableau so that the six before it and the six following give the play a symmetrical shape. There is a further principle of organisation: seven of the thirteen tableaux are in the form of dream episodes – or visions – which comment dramatically on the theme of the play as exposed in the other, realistically presented, tableaux. In these dream episodes where Friedrich appears as different characters, the action is often grotesque, even surrealistic. While these scenes are loosely linked to the play from a formal point of view, they are very effective in suggesting the gradual development of Friedrich's transformation into a new man. They also serve another purpose: Friedrich's assumption of various roles – that of a soldier, an onlooker in the hospital, a priest, a prostitute's customer, a prisoner, a wanderer, a mountain climber – not only illustrates the various stages of a man's life but also suggests that Friedrich is Everyman, and that misguided mankind will rise again after undergoing a kind of historical crucifixion. Friedrich is a Christ figure (the stages he goes through suggest the Stations of the Cross) who is destined to lead mankind through a peaceful revolution into a New Age of liberty and justice. Toller uses a heightened poetic speech in the dream episodes to provide contrast with the more prosaic language employed in the realistic tableaux.

The plot of such a play is best understood by following the various stations since the psychological course of the protagonist is reflected in the play's architectonics. *Die Wandlung* opens with a prologue which, while a fascinating scene in its own right, is only loosely linked to the action of the play. This may be the reason why Toller indicated that it could also be used as an epilogue. In this prologue, called 'The Barracks of the Dead', Death-by-War argues with Death-by-Peace in a military cemetery about who is superior. Death-by-Peace wins the debate.

The first *Station* is divided into two tableaux (*Bilder*), one realistic, the other dreamlike. In the realistic one a young Jew, Friedrich, is torn by his feeling of not belonging, of being eternally in search of a homeland like Ahasuerus, the wandering Jew whom he calls his brother. For Friedrich the Christians, celebrating the birth of Christ, are more attractive than the members of his family who, in his eyes, not only are outcasts but also represent the bourgeois middle class in their rigid, narrow-minded morals and outdated values. Like many of the young Expressionist writers he scorned his own background because he considered it reactionary, racist and materialistic. Friedrich's mother stands for the whole class:

MOTHER: . . . Meanwhile I have just one thing to ask you, a tiny favour – just to please your old mother. Friedrich, I beg you to attend Divine Worship. People would be so . . .

FRIEDRICH: People! Why not be honest and call it Public Service, not Divine? What is your God but a cruel and narrow judge, judging all men by cut and dried laws. Judging always by the same dead laws. Divine Service – homage to bigotry! It's revolting! (S.P. 64)

In his bitterness, Friedrich asserts that he is strong enough to live alone; he rejects his friend and the friend's sister, Gabriele, since he wants to spare her the embarrassment of being seen in the company of a Jew. He is overjoyed when he learns that volunteers are needed to fight a colonial war. He joins for two reasons: firstly, he believes that war will be heroic and signal the birth of a new era where there will be no more barriers between classes or religions; secondly, he wants to prove that he belongs to the others, that he is a German. Toller deliberately chooses the eve of Christmas, symbol of peace and love, to emphasise the wrongness of Friedrich's choice. Like Bertolt Brecht's *Trommeln in der Nacht* (*Drums in the Night*), 1922, *Die Wandlung* dramatises an undefined colonial war to reinforce Toller's conviction that *any* war is evil.

The dream episode entitled 'Troop-train' is reminiscent of Toller's own journey from Alsace to the war front: '*Compartment of a travelling troop-train. Badly burning oil-lamps shed a meagre, flickering light on the sleeping* SOLDIERS *huddled close together. With them one silent soldier (with* FRIEDRICH'S *features) and another with a skull for a head: both shadowy figures*' (S.P. 66). The purpose of this scene is to contrast Friedrich's naiveté with the harsh reality of war. The two soldiers listen while seven soldiers in a choric lament speak of the horrors they have encountered.

The second *Station* is again divided into two tableaux, one realistic, one dreamlike. Toller cleverly translates the soldiers' lament into the actual horrors of a battlefield where Friedrich encounters wounded and dying soldiers. The war-hardened soldiers mock the Fatherland with which Friedrich wishes to identify himself; he will never have a homeland, they jeer, because they are *all* without a homeland. Friedrich, as if to postpone making a decision, volunteers for a suicide mission.

The dream episode of this *Station* called 'In the Barbed Wire Entanglements' is probably the most expressive scene of the play; the stage directions read: '*Dark clouds sweep across the face of the moon. To right and left are barbed-wire entanglements in which hang skeletons white with quicklime. The earth is torn up with craters and shell-holes*' (S.P. 70). In the *danse macabre* that now takes place the skeletons dance to music provided by the rattling of the amputated leg-bones of other skeletal soldiers. The point is made that death reduces all men to a common denominator: there is no difference between black and white, between simple soldiers and officers. Typically, Toller tempers the cynicism of the scene by introducing a thirteen-year old girl (also a skeleton) who had died

26

because of a mass rape; her appearance provides an emotional element which heightens the macabre aspects of the scene. Neither Kaiser nor the early Brecht used this method of relating unlike emotions (cynicism and pathos) although Brecht later realised its effectiveness and – defying his own theories – applied it in *Mutter Courage* where Courage sings a cradle song as she rocks the dead Kattrin, and in *Der gute Mensche von Sezuan* (*The Good Person of Szechwan*) where Shen-Te shows her unborn son the beauties of the world. This is the only scene of *Die Wandlung* in which Friedrich is not present; it is meant to deliver a universal message (Toller's personal view) about the absurdity and horror of war; despite the fact that it is a dream episode, the 'reality' of this scene is shockingly convincing.

The third *Station* is again divided into a realistic and a dream episode. Friedrich, the sole survivor of the suicide mission, lies in a military hospital in a state of shock. His wish to belong to the 'others' has come true but at a price of ten thousand war dead. For the first time he starts to question the validity of war: 'The jubilation in their faces! Ten thousand dead! Ten thousand have died that I may find a country. Why don't you laugh? Is that liberation? Is this a time of greatness? Are these the people of greatness? (*Staring rigidly before him.*) Now I am one of you' (S.P. 75). In the ensuing dream episode Friedrich appears as onlooker in a military hospital where a doctor (with a skull instead of a head) parades a number of amputees to whom he has given artificial limbs. Friedrich faints and in a vision within the vision learns of the desperate condition of these cripples:

SPINAL PATIENT: . . .You'd make a fuss if you'd been hit like me.

I'm used to it by now.
I hardly know to-day
Whether I am a man still or a living lavatory.
My bowels are blown to bits;
My heart's the only living thing about me . . .
Will no one here blow out my heart as well
and make a job of it?   (S.P. 77–8)

In a further metamorphosis, Friedrich appears as a priest to bring them the word of the 'Saviour' but the sight of the cripples belies his hollow words. Realising the hypocrisy of his position he breaks the cross. This represents another step towards Friedrich's transformation; the old doctrines are dead, new ones have to be established to relieve mankind from unjust and unjustified suffering:

PRIEST: . . .
    Oh Christ, how are your teachings mocked!
    There is no healing,
    I see no light
    To light this endless night;
    Nowhere a guiding hand.
    Prepare for your salvation . . .
    How could I, myself in need of consolation,
    In bitterer need than you,
    Dole comfort on you?
    I can no more;
    Now I walk with you, at your head . . .
                                    (S.P. 79–80)

This scene establishes the first suggestion that Friedrich will grow into the saviour role once more replacing the old Adam by a Christ-like figure. One detail in the sixth tableau remains to be mentioned: not only has the skull-

28

headed doctor given the crippled soldiers artificial limbs, he has also constructed a special mechanism which enables those who were castrated once again 'to multiply and relish the joys of marriage'. This theme of castration with which Toller was preoccupied becomes a central concern in his play *Hinkemann*; *Die Wandlung* provides several hints that Friedrich may have suffered a similar fate.

The fourth *Station* consists of only one tableau, the climactic seventh, climactic in that it represents Friedrich's transformation into a New Man. He is now a sculptor, working on a statue of a man who stands with clenched fists in defence of his homeland. Friedrich's doubts about his creativity express symbolically his doubts about patriotism and warfare. These doubts change to despair when Gabriele rejects him (on the order of her parents) because he is a Jew, he who had tried so desperately to become a German. War and its futility are further illustrated in Friedrich's encounter with a beggar woman and her husband who are ravaged by syphilis contracted in a colonial war. Stricken, he cries out:

> Can a country really ask this much of us? Or has our country sold its soul, sold it to the State? Perhaps the State is a pimp, and our country a whore to be sold for any brutal lust – blessed by that procuress, the Church! Can a Fatherland that asks so much really be divine? Can it be worth the sacrifice of a single soul? (S.P. 85)

He destroys the statue and is about to shoot himself when his sister enters and reveals to him his ultimate destiny:

> SISTER: . . . I will shield your eyes; then you will see.
> Your path leads to God.
> . . .

29

To God, who is spirit, love and strength;
To God who dwells in the heart of humanity.
Your path will lead to humanity.   (S.P. 86)

Throughout *Die Wandlung* Toller uses religious images
and symbols, especially that of the cross. These symbols
force Friedrich to realise how much the Christian message
of love for mankind and Christ's sacrifice have been
distorted in the course of history. For example, on a
spy-mission Friedrich had been captured and tied to a tree
which in his delirium he takes for the cross, now symbolic of
the *useless* sacrifice of so many soldiers. A Red Cross nurse
who wears a cross on her uniform rejoices that with God's
help ten thousand enemy soldiers have been killed. The
war decoration through which he is finally accepted as one
of 'the others' is in the form of a cross. In his role as a priest
he breaks the cross. The next *Station* further exploits the
symbol of the cross; however, it now begins to suggest
resurrection rather than death, in keeping with the theme
of Friedrich's transformation.

The fifth *Station* consists of three tightly linked dream
episodes (tableaux eight, nine and ten) and the realistic
eleventh tableau in which Friedrich begins to establish
himself as leader of the people. The preceding dream
episodes can be considered as Friedrich's course through
the unenlightened stages of life followed by death and
resurrection, which is the title of the ninth tableau. The
action in tableaux eight to ten is to be understood as taking
place in Friedrich's mind, and it is Toller's commentary on
his conviction that the possibility of the birth of a better
human kind exists. The theme is almost identical to
Kaiser's as expressed in *Hölle, Weg, Erde* (*Hell, Way,
Earth*), 1919.

In the eighth tableau Friedrich, the customer of a young

prostitute, kills her demented mother out of mercy so that the girl's younger brothers and sisters can be sent to an orphanage where they will be better cared for. The ninth tableau presents Friedrich as a prisoner. After a suicide attempt he is found lying on the ground 'his head bent backwards, his arms outstretched as if crucified'. He is tried by judges who again wear skulls instead of heads. In this dream vision Friedrich, in his role as prisoner, meets with his wife who is pregnant with their child. The scene suggests that the fathering of a child may be a curse since, in his opinion, men are born only to suffer and be crucified. But there is also the suggestion that pain and death are necessary to achieve a higher life:

> Perhaps through crucifixion only
> Liberation comes;
> Perhaps the powers of light
> Spring only from His blood.
> Perhaps through crucifixion only
> Can redemption come,
> The way to light and freedom. (S.P. 93)

Friedrich dies and his wife gives birth to a child in a scene that is invested with allusions to the birth of Christ: the child is born in poverty, the other prisoners come to adore it, the air is filled with music and floods of sunlight, while the prison roof 'vaults into an infinite sky'. (The guarded note of optimism sounded in this tableau gives way, in Toller's later plays, to an ever increasing pessimism. In the later plays his protagonists are either killed or – more often – commit suicide.)

In the tenth tableau Friedrich is a wanderer now sure of his destination. The language is rich with echoes of Christ's resurrection:

THE WANDERER: I feel to-day as though
    This were a new awakening.
    As though the grave has split asunder
    And shown the sky again.
    The earth chained vessel breaks.
    Judge is now prisoner,
    And prisoner judge;
    And both stretch out their hands,
    Casting aside their triumphs and their shames
    Like crowns of thorns. (S.P. 94)

The eleventh tableau takes place at a public meeting of the working class to which four speakers have been invited: an anti-pacifist, a university professor, a priest and a political demagogue. The scene is an outspoken satire on the existing class system: each class is depicted as being primarily selfish; not only have they lost the ability to communicate with each other but they are totally incapable of recognising the need of hungry people. The workers, in turn, are most attracted by the demagogue who preaches bloody revolution as the final solution to their plight. At this point Friedrich demands to be heard. The theme of his address, much elaborated in the thirteenth tableau, can be considered a leitmotif of Toller's works:

I am not speaking of material want, my friends. It is not right that you should suffer hunger. I wish you bodily comfort and spiritual want. I wish you this in the name of the love that unites us all. You must no longer starve. You must be rich, you must find your life's fulfilment. I will fight side by side with you against poverty and misery. (S.P. 97)

The last *Station* begins with a dream episode in which

32

Friedrich and his friend appear in the role of mountain climbers. The friend, however, cannot follow Friedrich to the mountain top, symbolically the height of his mission as leader of the people and also the climax of his transformation into a new man.

In the final tableau Friedrich meets his mother, his uncle, and the doctor who reject his vision of a new and better world in which race, religion and fatherland are superseded by a worldwide community of working people. Only his sister approves of his course. In a final ecstatic speech he wins the workers over to his vision; they too undergo a transfiguration:

> Go to the soldiers and tell them to beat their swords into ploughshares. Go to the rich and show them your heart, your heart that was once buried alive beneath their rubbish. Yet be kind to them, for they too are poor, poor and straying. But the castles – these you must destroy; destroy them laughing, the false castles of illusion. Now march! March forward in the light of day ... (*All the people are now standing with outstretched hands. Then they join hands and march away.*)
>
> ALL: Brothers, stretch out your tortured hands
> With cries of radiant, ringing joy!
> Stride freely through our liberated land
> With cries of Revolution, Revolution! (S.P. 105–6)

In 1930, looking back on *Die Wandlung*, Toller wrote: 'Every author wants to press into his first work his whole knowledge of all his experience. I did the same. It is not surprising therefore that private and lyrical elements are more prevalent than the dramatic architectonic would permit' (T. 1/138–9). He admits also that the dramas written in prison suffer from lack of discipline because in his confined situation his works were the only means by which he could test and discuss his ideas or vent his frustrations. Certainly *Die Wandlung* has a number of weaknesses. Friedrich has no real antagonist, there is no conflict to be solved; he goes through a learning process which makes him accept what, in reality, he has always been. Consequently, the transformation, in itself a weak scene, does not bring about a true change of character; he only realises that the course pointed out by his sister is the best one for him to choose. Then, too, the transformation of the hungry and miserable workers from angry would-be revolutionaries into an all-embracing brotherhood of mankind is unconvincing and unrealistic. Toller's idealism here borders on the naive. His style is still inconsistent; in its worst passages it is reminiscent of the young Schiller, the pathos is too thick, even pompous.

Despite these flaws this *Stationendrama* is one of the best of its kind; inner and outer structure are intrinsically linked together; the psychological process of the protagonist's development is made 'visible' through a generally dynamic imagery and language. The play also already anticipates the political theatre of the 1920s culminating in the Piscator production in 1927 of Toller's *Hoppla, wir leben!*

The premiere of *Die Wandlung* took place on 30 September 1919 at the Tribüne, and according to contemporary accounts the fluidity of the play's form and Toller's anguished concern with topical issues were strikingly mirrored in the production. The theatre had just been founded by the up-and-coming director Karlheinz Martin who planned to promote Expressionism in Berlin. The theatre's seating capacity was just under three hundred and, as it was located in the elegant district of Berlin-Charlottenburg, its seat prices, ironically, were out of reach of the blue-collar workers for whom *Die Wandlung* in particular was intended. The stage was small without any elaborate stage machinery; there was no curtain since Martin wanted to create as intimate a contact between audience and action on stage as possible; scene endings were indicated by blackouts.[1] Because of its smallness, Martin could not work with the divided stage which the play required for its dream visions. The stage designer, Robert Neppach, solved the problem by creating a two-dimensional stage, avoiding the illusion of perspective; his material was basically colour applied to movable flat cubist forms against a black background. Paul Weiglin reports:

> The decoration in every tableau consists of nothing more than a simple partition set, painted by Robert Neppach in that expressionist style which reminds us of paintings by children's hands because of its unconcerned manner and perspective. A bit of a wall with a lopsided window: a room; a white-blue wall: a military hospital; some yellow with a suggestion of a shell-hole: a battlefield – that's all, and it is indeed sufficient.[2]

Neppach's ingenious design, comparable to that of the *Stilbühne* (stylised stage), not only opened the way to abstract stage design but also abolished the use of conventional props and influenced the actor's movements and gestures. Furthermore, it reinforced the principles of modern staging: to *activate* the public's imagination, in contrast to the naturalist *Illusionsbühne* (the theatre of illusion). Martin emphasised lighting techniques which had been employed by Max Reinhardt as early as 1917 in his production of Sorge's *Der Bettler* at the Deutsches Theater, Berlin. Sorge was fascinated by the *Simultanbühne* (simultaneous staging) and Reinhardt solved the problem of presenting simultaneous scenes by separating them through spotlights. Martin's extensive use of spotlighting was meant to highlight characters in a prominent and abstract manner; thus lighting was no longer used merely to illuminate the stage but as a directional aid in interpreting the play. Although Toller did not indicate that music was to be used in his play, Martin had W. R. Hagemann write a small score for violin to bridge scene changes.

Because of the small dimensions of the stage, Martin reduced crowds to a few characters whose movements and gestures were highly stylised. Herbert Jhering, one of Germany's most influential theatre critics, recorded his impressions of the performance, which he thought was among the most theatrical Berlin had to offer:

... A public meeting was not represented through masses but through accentuated groups. On that evening theatre moved a step forward. The Tribüne vindicated its aims. How the single characters were subservient to the idea of the whole! Bodies became ecstatic, voices explosive. A student ... through her forehead and chin, through her eye and hand transmitted such intensity in listening and understanding that her words became of secondary importance. Herr Gottowt, in his various appearances as Death, presented such a sharp, precise and accentuated image of the grotesque as to leave his romanticised beginnings in Reinhardt far behind.[3]

Fritz Kortner, who created the role of Friedrich, received equally high praise from the critics. He was to become one of Germany's most celebrated Expressionist actors.[4] Having been a pupil of Max Reinhardt and the choral leader in Reinhardt's production of *Oedipus Rex* he had been trained in diction as well as in statuesque gestures 'that were meant to project against gigantic staging areas'. When applied to the small stage of the Tribüne his larger-than-life style of acting had an overwhelming effect on the audience. His acting belonged in the category of the Expressionist *Ich*-performance which 'focused upon the single ecstatic-actor surrounded by or confronted with dozens of choral-performers who moved in unison, creating grotesque, but picturesque, poses'.[5]

Interestingly, most of the costumes were realistic in contrast to the abstract nature of the production; only the skeleton characters were stylised. They wore dark leotards which had bone shapes painted on them with fluorescent light; their faces were made up in black and white to suggest skulls.

Martin and his dramaturge, Rudolf Leonhard (himself an Expressionist writer and political revolutionary), edited and adapted the play to reflect Martin's preoccupation with the *Zentralidee* (central idea) of *Die Wandlung* which he identified with the play's subtitle – 'the struggle of a man'. The prologue, for example, was omitted. Stefan Gross-mann reports that the eighth tableau was followed by the eleventh (which Leonhard had shortened and combined with the also revised thirteenth).[6] The beginning of tableau nine, which now formed the end of the play, was omitted. The play therefore closed with the birth of the child (Friedrich, as prisoner, does not die) which was meant to symbolise the birth of the New Man. While the outcome of these changes may have been theatrically effective, they distorted the play's message because they weakened its cry for a peaceful revolution. A number of critics disagreed with Martin's editing; their praise, however, of his direction was unanimous and enthusiastic.

The collaboration of Martin and Neppach in the produc-tion of *Die Wandlung* proved highly successful (both were to continue to work together), and there is no doubt that their innovations in direction and stage design were in part responsible for the play's success. Since most of Toller's plays staged in Germany were produced by the most innovative theatre directors of the 1920s like Martin, Fehling or Piscator, a number of critics have attributed his success mainly to that fact. On the other hand, Toller's plays were often chosen by such directors because they lent themselves beautifully to innovative stage techniques.

'Masse Mensch' ('Masses and Man')

Toller wrote the first draft of *Masse Mensch* in October 1919, and he spent the following year rewriting the play, which he dedicated to the proletariat. It received its premiere on 29 September 1921 at the Volksbühne, Berlin, with Jürgen Fehling directing. In the preface to the second edition (1922), Toller addressed himself to Fehling on the relationship of his art and his politics because he felt the play had been misunderstood by the critics: 'In my political capacity, I proceed upon the assumption that units, groups, representatives of various social forces, various economic functions have a real existence; that certain relations between human beings are objective realities. As an artist, I recognise that the validity of these "facts" is highly questionable. ("It further remains to be determined whether we exist as individuals.")' (S.P. 111). In this preface Toller also expresses his view about proletarian art which, in his opinion, has a redemptive and liberating function: 'I need not dwell on the fact that proletarian art must ultimately rest on universal human themes. It can only exist where the creative artist reveals that which is eternally human in the spiritual characteristics of the working people' (S.P. 112).

The New Man: Birth and Crucifixion

As *Die Wandlung* is, in part, based on Toller's war experience, so *Masse Mensch* is, in part, based on Toller's role and experience in the Bavarian Revolution of 1919. The play's protagonist, Sonia Irene L., is modelled on the historical figure of Sonja Lerch,[7] but she also mirrors Toller in his role as a pacifist and revolutionary forced to recognise that he will commit violence in order to achieve his revolutionary purposes. *Masse Mensch* is the record of Toller's attempt to come to terms with his subsequent feelings of guilt. In an article entitled 'Man and the Masses: The Problem of Peace', Toller describes the issues that led him to write *Masse Mensch*:

Must the man of action always be dogged by guilt? Always? The masses, it seemed, were impelled by hunger and want, rather than by ideals. Would they still be able to conquer, if they renounced force for the sake of an ideal? Can a man not be an individual and a mass-man at one and the same time? ... As an individual a man will strive for his own ideals, even at the expense of the rest of the world. As a mass man, social impulses sweep him towards his goal, even though his ideals have been abandoned. The problem seemed to me insoluble. I had come up against it in my own life, and I sought to solve it. It was the conflict that inspired my play, *Man and the Masses*.   (T. 1/78)

Masse Mensch like *Die Wandlung* is a *Stationendrama* in that it portrays the various stages of Sonia's political and psychological development which is sparked by her participation in the revolution. (In the play she is known as The Woman.) But Toller has given up the former division into *Stationen* while retaining the use of tableaux (the play consists of seven tableaux); furthermore, in contrast to *Die*

39

Wandlung, he does not make a clear distinction between realistic and dream episodes. As he states in the preface: 'These pictures of "reality" are not realism, are not local colour; the protagonists (except for Sonia) are not individual characters. Such a play can only have a spiritual, never a concrete, reality' (S.P. 111).

Tableaux two, four and six are *Traumbilder* (dream pictures whose stage directions are only 'indicated', meaning that they were to be abstract rather than realistic), while tableaux three, five and seven are supposed to be *in visionärer Traumferne* (dreamlike visionary projections) although, in fact, they develop the 'realistic' content of the play.

The first tableau introduces Sonia Irene L. (Irene, like Friedrich, means peace) as the leader of revolutionary workers on the eve of a battle against their employers. She is joined by her Husband who is totally opposed to her political activities because it would damage his career as a government official. Torn between her love for him and her conviction that her political and moral concepts are right, she makes love to him for a final time.

The second tableau is a grotesque parody of a bankers' meeting at the Stock Exchange. In order to stimulate the weary soldiers the bankers come up with the idea of establishing a State-subsidised brothel disguised as a sanatorium, and all they propose for the survivors of a mine disaster is a charity dance:

THE BANKERS: We will contribute,
    We will dance,
    The proceeds go
    To the poor!
    (*Music of clinking gold coins.* THE BANKERS *in top-hats dance a fox-trot round the desk*.)   (S.P. 126)

This scene, with its abstract language and depiction of the Bankers' cynical bargaining, echoes the style of Kaiser's *Gas* plays. However, as in the skeletons' dance scene from *Die Wandlung*, Toller again introduces an emotional element by having the Woman remind them that they bargain with human lives:

THE WOMAN (*softly*): Gentlemen,
These are men and women.
I say again
Are *men* and *women*.   (S.P. 125)

While Kaiser remains an uninvolved, distanced observer in his plays, Toller repeatedly raises moral questions and comments on them through his *personae*.

The third tableau opens with a lament from a chorus of the masses which, in abstract manner, depicts the plight of the poor. The lament is picked up by various groups of workers who direct their anger at ruthless manufacturers and industrialists. The Woman opposes their decision to destroy the factories; although she is as opposed to industrial exploitation as the proletariat, she prefers a peaceful and passive course of action:

Hear me: I call strike!
Who henceforth feeds munition works,
Betrays his brother –
More than betrays –
Slays his own brother!
And you, women!
Remember the old legend
Of women stricken with eternal barrenness
For forging arms!
Think of your men who suffer!
I call a strike!   (S.P. 130)

41

At this point where she wins over the workers, Toller introduces a character called the Nameless. While *Die Wandlung* ends on a call for peaceful revolution, *Masse Mensch*, through the introduction of an antagonist and the ensuing conflict, explores the issue further and in more dramatic fashion. The Nameless, who is equally opposed to the exploitation of the working classes by capitalism, wants a 'last, reckless battle'. He calls for a *bloody* revolution. His weapon against the Woman is the fact that he is one of the workers, while the Woman is an outsider, a bourgeois. He is the masses. Although her conscience tells her that he is wrong, his argument is so persuasive and seductive that the Woman falls prey to it. She will remain silent during the ensuing battle.

The fourth tableau (a dream picture) is another of Toller's *danses macabres*. It takes place at night in a prison-like surrounding as the guards sing an eerie song about their childhood and adult life in the gutter. The Nameless, here an allegorical figure of Death, begins to play wildly on a concertina and invites them to a *Totentanz* (dance of death). The Woman appears and discovers to her horror that her husband is among the prisoners to be executed; her desperate pleas for mercy are sarcastically rejected. The scene ends with the Woman standing at the side of her Husband. In this tableau Toller establishes the conflict between the individual and the mass through an interesting device. The face of the Prisoner (Husband) suddenly metamorphoses into that of a guard, to suggest that their humanity transcends their roles. However, the Woman's realisation that 'Only Man counts' is refuted by the guard's assertion that 'Only the Masses count'. At this point her inner struggle begins. It centres upon the problem Toller had encountered himself: 'What happens when people, who are absolute pacifists and not only abhor violence but even force, come in contact with this destructive will and permit it full reign? The moral plane of the single individual is one thing, the political plane of masses and peoples another' (T. 1/82).

Depicting the final stage of the workers' revolutionary battle, the fifth tableau is obviously modelled on the fighting in Munich in 1919 between members of the third soviet republic and the troops sent in by the Hoffmann government. Various workers interrupt a dialogue between the Woman and the Nameless with reports that they are losing the battle. In vain, the Woman tries to prevent more bloodshed; the Nameless defeats all her attempts; he goes so far as to turn the masses against her as a traitress so that he can arrest her. The scene ends on a climactic note as the Nameless not only betrays the Woman but abandons his people as well just before the military enter the assembly hall. As the workers, at the conclusion of the fifth tableau, begin to intone the *Internationale* (the song [*Lied*] is given the function of a *dramatis persona*), it is cut off by machine-gun fire.

In the sixth tableau, perhaps the most intimate and complex of the play, Toller explores the Woman's guilt, which is the guilt of the idealist condemned to inaction. The Woman is first accused by headless shadows – the dead of the revolution – of being a murderer because she had kept silent and thus caused their death. The Woman, who wants to identify herself with the masses, tries to discover why humanity is enslaved. To her cry that 'Masses are fate, Masses are guiltless', the prison guard replies: 'Man is guiltless'. When she is driven to denounce God as the principle of guilt, the guard retorts: 'God is in you'. The Woman, forced to recognise that the struggle is interior, that mankind's ills are not due to external forces, and that liberation can only be achieved by mankind's own

43

endeavours, now attains an ambiguous freedom (her handcuffs symbolise that she is indeed a prisoner of her nature):

THE PRISONER: I am free?
THE WARDER: Unfree!
　　Free! (S.P. 146)

The seventh tableau elaborates on the ambiguous conflict between man and masses, between the conflict of economic and human interests:

THE WOMAN: . . .
　　O cleft and struggle of all living!
　　Welded to husband – welded to work.
　　To husband – to foe . . .
　　To foe?
　　Bound to the foe?
　　Bound to myself? . . .
　　That he would come. I need conviction. (S.P. 147)

The ensuing conversation with her Husband makes her aware of the unbridgeable gap between their differing political concepts. He serves the State and therefore considers any upheaval of the masses dangerous and evil. She accuses him of being a servant of this State and thus responsible for the proletariat's living conditions and for their revolution. As an individual the Woman wants her Husband's love; as a member of the masses, she now sees clearly that they have been misled by the Nameless and, believing that one day a peaceful union of individual men will be established, she offers her hand to her Husband as her brother. As she had anticipated, he refuses; the time is not ripe yet for her kind of vision. The Nameless comes to offer her escape from prison but she refuses because he would have to kill a prison guard.

In their last vehement dialogue, which centres upon the question of whether the aim justifies the means, his ruthless pragmatism clashes violently with her idealistic vision of the essential goodness in mankind which can be brought to light in a gradual and peaceful process of development:

> THE WOMAN: No, you do not love people!
> THE NAMELESS: Our Cause comes first.
> I love the people that shall be,
> I love the future.
> THE WOMAN: People come first.
> You sacrifice to dogmas,
> The people that are now.
> THE NAMELESS: Our Cause demands their sacrifice.
> But you betray the Masses, you betray
> The Cause. (S.P. 151)

To his further reproach that she lives in the future and lacks the courage to act she retorts idealistically that while he lived yesterday and lives today he will die tomorrow; she, however, will live eternally. Having rejected her Husband and the Nameless she finally rejects the Priest whose hollow phrases could never be of any comfort to her. Her last credo is dictated by her love for mankind and not for God. She chooses death because a guard would have to be killed if she fled. The play ends on a note of hope. Two women prisoners who had impulsively stolen the Woman's belongings begin to reflect remorsefully when they hear the firing squad: 'Sister, why do we do such things?' (S.P. 154).

While *Masse Mensch* resembles *Die Wandlung* in structure and in the characters, the themes of transformation into a better self and of uniting mankind under a reign of peace and justice have undergone considerable change and development. Toller's political experiences obviously contributed to a change in attitude. As he writes: 'I was a convinced pacifist, but reality set me right' (T. 1/82). The reality he encountered has been dramatised in the character of the Nameless who, while a demagogue, is also a realist whose logic is hard to refute. His argument is based on facts against which the Woman can oppose only her own ethical and moral convictions and idealistic and futurist vision. Toller quite clearly condemns the attitude of the Nameless, but he had also come to realise that an uncritical and passive idealism will not necessarily bring about change. The Woman's death is totally useless to the hungry masses; it is the death of a martyr. It may even be said that it merely reconciles her with her own ideals. The play does not solve the dilemma arising from the individual's conviction that human life is sacrosanct and the belief of the masses that it may be sacrificed.

The most interesting feature of *Masse Mensch* is Toller's attempt to develop a socialist theory which depicts almost in German classical fashion man's possibility of developing into a greater human being through suffering. His theory is radical in that it rejects any form of violence in this process of development. *Masse Mensch* also displays Toller's changing image of the New Man of the Expressionist tradition. A letter to his friend Tessa on 18 May 1921 sums up more explicitly what can already be sensed in the play: 'I do not believe any longer in a transformation to a "new" mankind. Every change is some kind of metamorphosis. I perceive more deeply than ever the meaning of the tragic yet merciful saying: Man becomes what he already is' (T. 5/66).

The play was premiered on 15 November 1920 in the Stadttheater of Nürnberg, directed by Friedrich Neubauer.

Since the Bavarian government considered it too political, the general public was not admitted and therefore the repercussion was small. The press reviews were mixed. It was the production at the Berlin Volksbühne on 20 September 1921 which became memorable and established Jürgen Fehling as Germany's most gifted director of Expressionist drama. Piscator had originally planned to stage the play in 1920 at his Proletarisches Theater in Berlin but found that it did not suit the political aims of his theatre well enough; he also disliked the play's 'fragmentary structure' and its 'wordy' style.[8] Jürgen Fehling, however, was fascinated by the play's possibilities, and his production was an overwhelming success with international repercussions. A contemporary observer, Kenneth Macgowan, who in 1921 took a ten-week trip through the theatres of Europe, was so impressed by Fehling's production as well as by the play that he ventured the prophecy that this director might 'become the leader of the new forces in the Continental theatre'. His eye-witness report combined with Robert Jones' sketches provides a detailed and lively picture of the play which featured Reinhardt's former pupil Mary Dietrich as Sonia. Appropriately Dietrich interpreted the character of the Woman as a Christlike figure.

Fehling's designer, Hans Strohbach, employed abstract and Expressionist 'props' in the style of Neppach. Macgowan notes his use of high black folds of curtains: 'For the dream scene, [2nd tableau] the stage is again in black curtains, but those at the rear are occasionally opened to show a clerk on an impossibly high stool, writing on an impossibly high desk, almost in silhouette against the yellow-lighted dome'.[9] Toller's suggestion only to 'indicate' the scene's props in the dream picture was applied in all scenes. Fehling did not emphasise the distinctions between

47

dream and realistic episodes and one gathers from contemporary reviews that the dream tableaux conveyed perhaps a more emotionally intense atmosphere, which would be justified for those scenes. An example of this is the sixth tableau in which the Woman goes through the several stages of her guilt. Photographs of the production show Dietrich crouched in a small cage like a birdcage placed on a platform from which a few steps lead upwards; beside her stands a towering guard. The impact of the scene lay in its exaggeration: the smallness of the cage in which the Woman cannot stand erect, the impression of an immense void around her created through blacking out the rest of the stage, the slow and precise movement of the accusing shadows – the bankers and prisoners.

Fehling was especially gifted in his direction of crowd scenes for which he made use of the *Jessnertreppen* and of intersecting light beams (he became famous for his *Licht-regie*, direction by means of lighting). In the fourth tableau, for example, green lanterns over which the prison guards hung emphasised their emaciated looks. The dance of death was highlighted by a sudden deep red light in the sky which 'pulses in and out', anticipating strobe-light effects. Macgowan's description of the fifth tableau, which ends in the defeat of the workers, gives a lively impression of Fehling's direction:

The stage is again boxed in black. There are steps like the corner of a pyramid rising up to the right of the audience. Upon these steps gather the working people. You see a host, affrighted and cowering, in the twenty-four men and women who stagger upon the steps singing 'The Marseillaise'. As they sway, locked together hand in hand, like men on a sinking ship, and the old song mounts up against the distant rattle of machine guns, the scene

48

brings the cold sweat of desperate excitement to the audience that fills the Volksbühne, . . . Suddenly there is a louder rattle of arms. The noise sweeps through the air. It drives into the souls of the huddling men and women. They collapse, go down, fall in a tangled heap. The curtains at the left loop up suddenly. There in the gap against the yellow sky stand the soldiers.[10]

Like *Die Wandlung*, *Masse Mensch* was an immediate success and again this was attributed to the production rather than to the play itself. Yet Fehling stated repeatedly that the success of *Masse Mensch* was due to Toller's merit as 'a social writer and a poet'. And the contemporary theatre critic, Alfred Kerr, while having some reservations about the play, nevertheless regarded Toller as 'the only Expressionist playwright who knows how to handle his genre'.

'Die Maschinenstürmer' ('The Machine-Wreckers')

Die Maschinenstürmer was written in the winter of 1920/21 in Niederschönenfeld prison. It differs somewhat from Toller's first two plays not only because it presents itself as an historical drama but also because Toller had read extensively for it. On 7 February 1921 he wrote to Gustav Mayer:

I found some more material for *Die Maschinenstürmer* in Marx's *Kapital* and in Engel's *Lage der arbeitenden Klasse in England* . . . In my play also, the machine is of more than material significance. It is 'devil', 'demon'; it is not only the social misery it creates (unemployment among the men, the sweat system, work division) which leads to its destruction but also its 'ghostly appearance'.

> And, finally, I have tried to turn the machine into a
> symbol of our mechanistic era.   (T. 5/60)

Perhaps because *Die Maschinenstürmer* is an historical play
it is more traditional in structure and plot development
than the earlier plays, although a number of elements and
themes from *Die Wandlung* and *Masse Mensch* have been
retained.

The drama takes place about 1815 at the time of the
Luddite movement in England. It consists of a prologue
and five acts; there are no dream scenes, although the
second scene of Act Five in its eerie and visionary nature is
reminiscent of Toller's former dream episodes. It is from
this play on that all Toller's *dramatis personae* have proper
names. The prologue depicts a debate in the British
Parliament as the House of Lords prepares to vote on a new
bill according to which anyone convicted of destroying
weaving machines would be punished by death. The Lord
Chancellor and his peers defend their theory that poverty
must not be eased because it is a law of God and Nature.
Lack of food is Nature's means of controlling England's
surplus and poverty-stricken population. The only opposition comes from Lord Byron (Toller's mouthpiece) who
argues that all people are equal. His objections are met
with sneers; 'Poets may dwell on emotions', he is told, but
statesmen must follow 'reason'. The bill is passed. Toller's
suggestion that the characters of Lord Byron, and Jimmy
Cobbett, the play's protagonist, and those of Lord Castle-
reagh and the manufacturer Ure, Jimmy's antagonist, be
played by the same actors helps to establish a tighter link
between the prologue and the play.

The plot evolves around two days in the life of a group of
weavers during which a revolt against a new weaving
machine that had caused a mass lay-off takes place; it ends

with the wrecking of the machine and with the brutal
slaying of Jimmy Cobbett. Like Friedrich in *Die Wandlung*
and Sonia in *Masse Mensch*, Jimmy is an outsider who
preaches peaceful and passive tactics rather than violence,
and like the other two protagonists he wins the workers
over through his charismatic powers. He argues that the
machine should not be destroyed, that technology is here to
stay; if the workers use the machines intelligently they can
become their masters and cease to be their slaves. He asks
for patience while the workers strengthen their position
through the establishment of unions. His speech to the
rebellious weavers is a typical example of Toller's Expressionist style in his early plays – ecstatic, emotional,
visionary; it suited the *Ich*-performance perfectly:

> Brothers, join hands! Begin! Begin! Not I and I and I!
> No! World and we and thou and I! If you *will* the
> comradeship workers, it is yours!
> O, this winnowing will shake the chaff from your souls!
> The earth will sprout again! And the tyrant of machinery,
> conquered by your own creative spirit, will be your tool
> and your servant! (S.P. 20)

Carried away by Jimmy's enthusiasm the workers spon-
taneously elect him as their new leader, dismissing their old
one, John Wible.

In *Die Maschinenstürmer* Jimmy is opposed by three
antagonists – his brother, the manufacturer, and Wible,
each of whom wishes to destroy his power over the
weavers. Henry, his brother, hates Jimmy because he
represents the class Henry has left behind; he now works
for the manufacturer Ure and he identifies himself with the
manufacturer's values, thus denying his own roots. When
Ure sets one brother to spy upon the other it is a further

image of the division among the working classes. Ure himself represents the ruthless but intelligent industrial manager; although he is attracted by Jimmy's courage and outspokenness – he even asks Jimmy to work for him – he ultimately refuses to give in to Jimmy's reasoning. His principle is expediency which guarantees profit, not pity with the poor. The scene in which Jimmy pleads with Ure on behalf of the workers is obviously modelled on the encounter between Marquis von Posa and King Philippe II in Schiller's *Don Carlos* where Posa pleads for freedom of thought for the King's subjects. Many Expressionist writers were indebted to Schiller, but unfortunately Toller's style is *too* reminiscent of him; it also exhausts itself in repetitive phrases, and at times the imagery is embarrassingly over-charged:

> JIMMY: Within our breast there is a bud
>   That longs to be unfolded, hiding wonder
>   On wonder in its petals. It is Thou!
>   That Thou can lift the Scriptural curse of toil,
>   And what is now our scourge, our brand of bondage
>   Shall be again our holy, happy task!   (S.P. 35)

Jimmy's language is that of a religious zealot and dreamer, and the down-to-earth task of creating a workers' union is constantly undermined by his vision of an all-loving, united humanity. As a consequence, John Wible, his third antagonist, has an easy game winning the hungry weavers back to him. Like the Nameless in *Masse Mensch* he calls for destructive action; like him he is a ruthless but realistic observer of the proletariat: 'Hunt them from their lairs like wild beasts! Blood is the lash to whip them out of sloth' (S.P. 25). And like the Nameless who attacked Sonia

52

for not belonging to the workers, Wible attacks Jimmy as an outsider who, because of his education, is really of the bourgeois class: 'I've no book-learning, but we shall see who knows the workmen best. The working folk feel otherwise, think otherwise than you' (S.P. 25). The weavers finally desert Jimmy for Wible because they do not understand Jimmy's concept of socialism; their needs are pressing and immediate while his programme calls for a lengthy process of worker education which will entail more deprivation.

In his essay *Arbeiten* ('Works') Toller states that he intended to portray in *Die Maschinenstürmer* a modern type of the proletariat. While the uneducated proletarian of the nineteenth century 'suffered under the burden of his fate which was misery, exploitation, long hours of work, little pay, the proletarian of the twentieth century turned into an active revolutionary in defence of an idea. He now not only criticises but pictures new realities which he wants to materialise' (T. 1/141–2). However, there is quite a discrepancy between Toller's intentions and their realisation in the play. In placing a twentieth-century proletarian (Jimmy) in a nineteenth-century milieu of uneducated workers, Toller distorts the history of trade unionism. Nowhere in the play does he take into account the fact that the formation of trade unions was made possible only with support from the middle-class bourgeoise which exercised a much greater pressure on Parliament, for example, than the proletariat. The teachings of Marx and Engels, both from well-to-do families, and of the very moderate Lassalle, did not influence the proletariat directly but through a number of middle-class citizens who fought the cause against opposition from industrial management and government. One can argue, of course, that because Jimmy can read and write he represents the middle-class citizen concerned with the fate of the proletariat, but Toller has not defined this clearly enough.

Jimmy's character lacks dramatic credibility because he advocates an ideology which Toller himself had started to doubt while working on *Die Maschinenstürmer*. In *Eine Jugend in Deutschland* he writes:

> I believed that the power of reason was so strong that he who had been taught rational behaviour would follow it. However, perceptions and experiences will always be forgotten, the development of the people is troublesome. Their deepest wounds are not afflicted by their enemy but by themselves.
>
> In my drama *Die Maschinenstürmer* I try to depict these very conflicts, the clash between revolutionaries and rebels, and also the fight of man against the machine which threatens his livelihood. . (T. 4/225)

The fight of the weavers against the machine is the central topic of the play and its strongest feature. While Jimmy is too patently a type of the New Man voicing a vision based on abstract concepts of altruism and denial, the weavers are psychologically well-defined and differentiated individuals who in their fear and need achieve a rich degree of humanity. It is this humanity which makes their fear of the machine so plausible. For them it is a monster, a Moloch demanding human sacrifice; symbolically it devours the hundreds of young children employed by Ure. Albert's vision of the machine becomes an apocalyptic vision of mankind's destruction:

> The greedy jaws of war will gape for men
> And nations will be fodder – brothers foes,
> And justice outlawed, order piled in dust!

The New Man: Birth and Crucifixion

Against their Mother Earth her children rise
To slay her creatures and uproot her woods,
Her godlike creatures and her godlike woods,
And shame her motherhood – the end is dust!

(S.P. 50)

'Always pursued, always crucified', Albert hangs himself.
(In the second version of the play the Engineer who tends
the machine hangs himself, having been driven mad by it.)

Albert's crucifixion, however, is not redemptive in any
way nor does it point towards the evolution of a New Man.
It points rather to man's degeneration and ultimate destruction. Toller disagrees with Marx's theory about the
benefits of technology; in *Die Maschinenstürmer* he voices
his concern about the inherent danger of it turning humans
into robots. This concern was shared by many writers of the
second half of the Expressionist period; the best example is
Kaiser's play *Gas II* where the workers in the gas manufac-
tory are reduced to 'skeletal' figures distinguishable only by
the colours of their uniforms. In the final scene the weavers
wreck the machine and beat Jimmy to death in the
mistaken belief that he has betrayed them. Ned Lud
expresses a vague hope that after them 'will come men
better school'd, more faithful, braver, to take up the fight'
(S.P. 53).

Toller never ceased to be sympathetic to the proletariat
but he came to see them more realistically. This shift in
attitude made him introduce two characters in the play who
act as mouthpieces of his new realism. These characters –
among his most ingenious creations – are the Beggar and
the Old Reaper. The Beggar's function can be compared
with that of the Shakespearean jester or fool. He is old and
wise but his wisdom is touched with cynical overtones. He is
well aware that the proletariat will not necessarily turn into

better human beings under better living conditions. He predicts accurately Jimmy's fate and the failure of his enterprise:

JIMMY: Working men keep faith.

BEGGAR: Some of them, maybe. But all? There's a question. Do all men keep their word, are all men brave and true? No. Then why working men? Because they work? Look at them as they are, and not as you would have them be.   (S.P. 42)

The figure of the Old Reaper is more complex and elusive than that of the Beggar. He is a Tiresias-like figure in his old age, with his young guide and his blind man's stick, but he also represents suffering humanity in search of God. The appalling suffering of industrial England (poignantly represented by his starving and crippled grandson, Teddy) makes him reject the God of conventional Christianity; he calls this God a 'Murderer of children' and he regards his stick as a gun with which he will shoot God. In an encounter with Jimmy, the Old Reaper suggests gnomically that the steam engine may be God:

OLD REAPER: Do you believe in the kingdom of God? The kingdom of Peace?

JIMMY: I fight as though I did.

OLD REAPER: Then tell me, where shall I find God?

JIMMY: I've never fallen in with Him. Maybe you'll find Him in yourself.

OLD REAPER: But aren't you fighting against God?

JIMMY: I fight as though I believed in Him.

OLD REAPER: He, he, he! The man's cracked! He fights against the engine, and doesn't know where God is!

Your wits have gone a wool-gathering, Jim. You'll
come to no good end. (S.P. 25)

In the play's final scene the identification is clearly made:

OLD REAPER: Is God in sight?
TEDDY: Here's the machine, grandfather.
OLD REAPER: The hour draws near. He is the engine! God
is the engine! (S.P. 53)

The Old Reaper recognises that the malevolent God, the
machine, can only be appeased with the lives of his victims –
the working class – now represented by the slain Jimmy.
The Old Reaper's final prayer, which is taken from the
Gospel, also suggests unmistakably the Christ-like nature
of Jimmy: 'Ah, poor dear Son! (*He bends weeping over
*JIMMY's *body and kisses it*.) And I will pray the Father, and
he shall give you another Comforter, even the Spirit of
truth' (S.P. 54). But his closing words intimate that the
future redeemer will again be crucified unless mankind
adopts his principles: '*man muss einander helfen und gut
sein*'. ('We must be good to one another.')

Die Maschinenstürmer has been compared to Gerhart
Hauptmann's *Die Weber* (*The Weavers*), 1883, because of
the similarity in topic, but the two plays differ substantially.
Unlike *Die Maschinenstürmer*, *Die Weber* is a truly historical drama about the successful revolt of a desperate group
of Silesian weavers against the manufacturer Dreissiger; its
naturalist style and imagery are in total contrast to Toller's
Expressionism. Toller himself denied any direct influence
of Hauptmann.

Die Maschinenstürmer, presented on 30 June 1922 in the
Grosses Schauspielhaus, Berlin, was once again directed by
Karlheinz Martin. After leaving Die Tribüne he had joined

the Proletarisches Theater which had been founded in early 1919. Its only performance in 1919 of Cranz's *Freiheit* (*Freedom*) had been a failure because of its 'Expressionistic idealism'. M. Patterson states: 'This "Proletarian Theatre" deservedly failed after its one performance. Martin could blame the indifference of the proletariat, but the real reason lay in the inability of ecstatic Expressionism to relate to the needs of working people'.[11]

Martin's designer was John Heartfield, who would also collaborate with Piscator in the production of *Hoppla, wir leben!* Because of the nature of the play, Heartfield's set had to be somewhat more realistic than were the sets for Toller's two previous plays. His gigantic machine towering over the masses of weavers conveyed accurately their fear of the 'monster'. Actor director Wilhelm Dieterle in the role of Jimmy was an overwhelming success, although the novelist Döblin noted his habit of 'milking' the public:

> Unending calls from the audience for Dieterle. He did not rise. He had been slain at the end, massacred, lay defeated on the ground of the arena. When the calling and the applause began, he did not rise. People at first believed that he continued to play his role. Then Granach – who played John Wible – starts talking to him; he does not rise. Granach runs back signalling others. They come and lift up the long man. He walks with difficulty. The house is quiet at once. All are standing; the stage, the arena is empty. After a tense minute some stagehands appear at the curtain. Then the curtain parts; Dieterle, supported by two of three men, staggers in; seems benumbed, half faint; is able to bow. Burst of applause, the clapping and calling last for minutes.
>
> (T. 6/138)

Since the stage of the Grosses Schauspielhaus was quite large Martin was able to introduce bigger crowd scenes than in *Die Wandlung*, but he remained faithful to his style of employing abstract movement. Once again most of the critics wrote favourably about the production but were less certain about the play itself. Stefan Grossman wished that Toller would 'abstain for three months from using certain words such as: Humanity, World-Community, Comrades, Slaves'. In his opinion the play should have been called, 'Ernst Toller's Collected Speeches' (T. 6/135–6). Grossman was also one of the critics who did not like Martin's production: 'He [Martin] has turned the play into an opera . . . Everything is as in a waxworks. He arranges tableaux and lets the characters remain motionless. Then, on a military command, the group is allowed to move, mostly by jerks. Martin's inanimate technique proved deadly for a play already so poor in spiritual life' (T. 6/137).

The fact that Toller was still in prison, and that Walther Rathenau, Minister for External Affairs, had been murdered on 24 June 1922 just a few days before the premiere, gave the production a topical and political significance out of all proportion to its historical theme. The audience called out Rathenau's name during the scene where Jimmy is slain by the mob. Ure was received with sneers. The public, Döblin noted, behaved like children in a puppet theatre. It seemed to be Toller's fate that his role as political agitator was forever overshadowing the artist. Frühwald sums it up: 'The performance of *Die Maschinenstürmer* distracted the public completely from all historical or literary questions; the fate of the imprisoned author, the fate of the murdered Rathenau stood in the foreground, seen as a parable for the fate of the Republic threatened from the Right' (T. 6/135).

The three plays, *Die Wandlung*, *Masse Mensch* and *Die*

Maschinenstürmer, constitute a cycle through which Toller explores the relationship of the individual worker to his class, his possible transformation into the New Man and the possibility of establishing a new peaceful socialist regime. With *Die Maschinenstürmer* these themes are exhausted. His next play, *Hinkemann*, begins Toller's second phase as a dramatist.

4
Man versus Society

'Hinkemann'

Hinkemann, written in 1921–22 in Niederschönenfeld prison, was intended by Toller as a social drama about the post-war misery of the German proletariat. In November 1921 he wrote to his friend Ernst Niekisch: 'The drafts of my latest drama . . . have given me a feeling of vocation: I believe that I can plough the field on which one day proletarian art will grow. . . . My Hinkemanns have the following annotation: Proletarian art, too, leads to humanity, it is all-embracing, like life, like death' (T. 6/117). The play was first called *Eugen Hinkemann* to indicate Toller's shift from writing another 'mass' drama to drama where the emphasis is on the individual character. In the first edition of 1923 the title was changed to *Der deutsche Hinkemann* but Toller, worrying justifiably that this new title might unduly emphasise the play as an allegory about Germany, gave it, in 1924, its final title – *Hinkemann*.

Despite the change of title the play, with its central

character an ex-German soldier emasculated in the First World War, was widely interpreted in right-wing circles as a libel on the myth of German virility and caused riots in the theatre. It was first presented without incident on 19 September 1923 in the Altes Theater in Leipzig, directed by Alwin Kronacher.[1] The critics agreed that the performance was a memorable theatrical event. The Dresden Staatstheater production under Paul Wiecke, however, instigated what came to be known as the *Hinkemann* scandals. In 1924 Germany's political parties were engaged in a power struggle that brought the country close to civil war and Toller, because of his political past, became the target of attacks from the right. During the Dresden performance of 17 January 1924, the eve of the celebration of the *Reichsgründungstag* (Foundation of the German Empire), an organised group of agitators from the German Nationalist Party and the National Socialist Party caused such a riot that the actors were barely able to finish the play and fighting broke out in the audience. The ringleaders among the rioters were arrested but were set free because the Court found they had acted in self-defence. A debate on 24 January in the Saxonian Parliament about the play ended inconclusively. *Hinkemann* had to be taken out of the repertoire because of death threats against actors and director. The threat to the actors was couched in the language of abuse that was to become standard with the National Socialist Party (the Nazis):

Has yesterday's theatre-scandal not been warning enough to you louts that you have the impudence to impose again on the respectable German public the Jewish concoction of a tramp and Bolshevist criminal whose place should be at the gallows and not in the theatre! . . .

The theatre is a public institution and belongs to the people! It is not a whorehouse where physically or mentally emasculated people, lavatory artists, or criminals can get away with celebrating their orgies.

(T. 6/146)

An anonymous pamphlet – Nazi-inspired – attacked *Hinkemann* as 'a play that mocks Christianity and German nationality, that ridicules our injured war heroes and whose imagery and language are mere filth' (T. 6/145).

Further performances of the play in 1924 in Vienna, Jena and Berlin were made possible only under strong police protection. The critics of the Berlin production, directed by Emil Lind and Erwin Berger with Heinrich George as Hinkemann and Renée Stobrawa as Grete, were divided; the negative reviews argued that the play was too sentimental and the topic of Hinkemann's emasculation against good taste. The positive reviews praised the play's dramatic structure, the treatment of the theme and the introduction of a Büchner-like proletarian protagonist as its strongest features.

Hinkemann, between 1923 and 1933, proved to be among Toller's most successful plays. It was staged in many European theatres, as well as in Russia and the United States. Toller himself directed the play in November 1927 at the Volksbühne in Berlin. Heinrich George played the role of Hinkemann once again and Helene Weigel, Brecht's wife, played the part of Grete. The play was banned by the Nazis and only in 1959 was it again staged for German audiences, now unfamiliar with the drama of the Expressionist period. Reaction, on the part of audiences and critics alike, was generally negative; one critic sums up the then prevalent attitude towards Expressionism in calling the play a remarkable work of literature comparable to Borchert's *Draussen vor der Tür* (*The Outsider*), 1946, 'despite its expressionistic pathos and looseness of structure'.[2]

Hinkemann, the only true proletarian figure Toller has created, is also his most powerful dramatic figure; Toller saw him as a tragic figure of his age:

> I dedicate this drama to you, nameless proletarian. To you, nameless hero of humanity; you are not mentioned in any book of fame, not in the history of revolutions or parties. Only an indifferent police-report in a corner of a newspaper under 'accidents and suicides' mentions you. Eugen Hinkemann stands symbolically for you. You have always suffered, in every society, under every government; branded by the dark fate you will have to suffer even then when in brighter times a socialist society will have been finally established. (T. 2/362)

The play is concerned primarily with Hinkemann's relationship with his wife, Grete. Although he has been emasculated in the war she still loves him. Wishing to buy her a Christmas gift and desperate for work, Hinkemann finally accepts a job in a carnival where he bites through the necks of live rats and drinks their blood because 'people like to see blood'. When, later, Hinkemann's friend, Grosshahn, seduces Grete he takes her to the carnival where they see Hinkemann performing. The booth owner introduces the 'act':

> Our last act (*points to Gene*) is Robot, the strong man of the Empire. Powerful as a grizzly bear. Devours live rats and mice before the very eyes of our esteemed public. The hero of the civilised world. The pride and power and manhood of the Empire. (S.P. 168)

Grete now realises that Hinkemann acts in this demeaning show because of his love for her. Overwhelmed by her feelings of shame and love she rejects Grosshahn. Later, in a small workers' pub, Hinkemann and a number of workers discuss the effects of the war on their lives. The workers' opinions are suggested by their names: Max Knatsch (the anarchist), Sebaldus Singegott (the preacher), Peter Immergleich (the indifferent one), Michel Unbeschwert (the carefree one). Grosshahn, drunk and hurt because Grete has rejected him, arrives and reveals the secret of Hinkemann's emasculation (learned from Grete); he further shames Hinkemann by stating falsely that Grete had found his carnival act ludicrous and disgusting. Hinkemann is devastated; his pain and the cruelty of his treatment are depicted in the next scene – Act Three, scene one – which portrays in staccato fashion the corruption and immorality of post-war Germany.

As Hinkemann lies in a faint in the middle of a city crowd newspaper boys shout their headlines; they scream of naked dancing, the slaughter of Jews, money dealings, syphilis, a new gas weapon, the collapse of the dollar. When Hinkemann returns to his dingy apartment he carries the statue of a priapus he had bought rather than the Christmas gift he had promised Grete. In the harrowing final scene Hinkemann and Grete are reconciled, but Grete is so appalled by her husband's profound despair that she commits suicide and the curtain descends on Hinkemann as he prepares to hang himself.[3]

In *Hinkemann* Toller is much more concerned with dramatising his ideas about man and society through the realistic and individualised characterisation of his protagonist who is seeking happiness for *himself* than with the abstract and universal types of his earlier plays who seek happiness for *mankind*. Hinkemann still symbolises the proletariat but Toller, as in *Die Maschinenstürmer*, has begun to create protagonists whose individuality is unmistakeable: psychological portraiture supersedes ideological didacticism. The reason for this change is that Toller had come to doubt the possibility that any social or political revolution could affect the mystery of human relationships or ameliorate the essential misery of the human condition. Both Hinkemann and Grete compare humans to insects caught in a spider's web: the comparison is reminiscent of that used by Lear in Shakespeare's darkest tragedy:

> As flies to wanton boys, are we to the gods:
> They kill us for their sport.

More than Toller's earlier plays, *Hinkemann* reflects the political and social scene in Germany in the early 1920s. In this play, however, Toller's attitude is more that of an observer who records objectively than that of a didact who believes that he can change the world. In the pub scene of Act Two, for example, several workers are involved in a discussion concerned mainly with their daily lives as workmen and husbands. Although they agree that Germany is in a political turmoil and that the gap between the proletariat and the rich bourgeoisie is growing, each character voices an individual and different opinion as to how to bring about a change for the better. There is no overall agreement any more, not even an attempt to reach one. Toller's abandonment of his earlier habit of depicting the proletariat as a *class* reflects the loss of his belief in the virtue of a class *per se*. In a letter to Stefan Zweig he writes:

> I have written the play at a time when I had become painfully aware of the tragic limits which even social revolution places on the experience of personal happi-

ness. It is the limit beyond which Nature is more powerful than the wishes of an individual or of society. Therefore, tragedy will never stop. Communism also has its tragedy. There will always be individuals whose suffering remains without a remedy. (T. 5/152)

Toller's more mature political and artistic discrimination led to surer and more authentic characterisation. The fact that Hinkemann is crippled may lead him to a better understanding of human nature and the human condition, but it does not turn him into a better person; he does not undergo a *Wandlung* triggered by experience or knowledge as was the case with Friedrich or the Woman. He is an anti-hero in his proletariat origins, in his drinking of rats' blood, in the brutality of his pessimism which drives Grete to commit suicide. In a letter to Paul Wiecke who had asked Toller whether Hinkemann was a tragic figure he replied: 'With Hinkemann I not only wanted to portray the unsolvable and therefore tragic suffering of a type who stands for many, but I also wanted to show the tragic limits of society where it cannot assist the individual any more' (T. 5/177).

In addition to Toller's change to more realistic characterisation, there is again – as in *Die Maschinenstürmer* – a change to a more traditional structure. The play is in five acts and its action is organised in a tighter fashion than in his earlier *Stationendramen*. However, the stage directions are rarely given in detail and for every scene are prefaced by the word: *Angedeutet* (best translated as 'suggested') because Toller, who was fascinated by the potential of modern staging, wished to avail himself of Expressionist stage techniques. Toller has also given up the dream scenes of his former plays which he used as a device to dramatise his ideology of man's transformation. The only scene still reminiscent of a dream episode occurs after Hinkemann's collapse in the street; this scene as well as the scene at the fair are already moving in the direction of 'theatrical insert' which Toller developed more fully in *Hoppla, wir leben!* His technique is to effect a montage-like assembling of catchwords (newspaper headlines) or quick-moving scenes developed by Piscator into the simultaneous film inserts of *Hoppla, wir leben!* Brecht would adopt this technique in order to comment on the action and to stimulate the spectator to become intellectually involved in the play's message. Further, the ideological monologues of the former plays have given way to dramatic dialogue. That the characters are usually at cross-purposes emphasises the tragedy of Hinkemann's solitude.

Hinkemann is not a typical Expressionist play in the line of playwrights like Sorge, Kaiser, Stramm or Hasenclever; the play belongs in the tradition of Realism. Its major influence is Büchner's *Woyzeck* (1836/37). Hinkemann, like Woyzeck, is a poor, uneducated creature trampled upon by society; both are haunted by voices; both are deeply affected by the unfaithfulness of the ones they love which results in their death. Marie and Grete both have recourse to religion when in despair. Grosshahn (big cock) is modelled on the 'manly' Tambourmajor. The scenes at the fair and in the pub also have precedents in *Woyzeck*. Büchner uses the words 'stab' and 'red' as leitmotifs to develop and explain why Woyzeck commits murder. Toller likewise introduces the laughter-ridicule motif to explain how Hinkemann is led to despair and suicide.

There is less use of symbolism in *Hinkemann* than in the earlier plays; Hinkemann (the name means the one who is incomplete[4]) is the most symbolic character in the play. Although Toller insisted that he should not be interpreted as an allegorical figure, contemporary German audiences were quite right to see correspondences between him and the crippled, defeated Germany of post-First World War in the same way that readers of Hemingway's *The Sun Also Rises* (1926) perceived the emasculated protagonist, Jake Barnes, to be a symbol of the post-war 'lost generation'. The emasculated Hinkemann may also represent the seer brought to realise the impossibility of begetting the New Man. This relates him to the goldfinch blinded by Hinkemann's mother so that it will sing better; Hinkemann draws the comparison himself before he kills the bird to shorten its agony:

> Poor little beast! Poor little blighter! They've fixed us up good and proper, you and me. Human beings did that. Human beings! If you could talk you'd say it was devils, what we call human beings. . . . Crumbs – and a cage. What, a cage? To show each other how miserable we are? No *I* won't be cruel to you. I'll be what they call Fate. Kinder than my fate is to me.　　(S.P. 160)

Grete is unable to offer Hinkemann any hope. Her name (the short form of Margarete) is commonly associated in Germany with a sweet, naive young woman with few brains (*das deutsche Gretchen*). She is trapped in a net of society's clichés which she accepts willingly. But her unquestioning and naive acceptance of God is of little help to her in time of crisis. She feels that God has destined her to love Hinkemann, and when he rejects her she can only commit suicide. It has been argued that Grete's love for Hinkemann is a form of *caritas* (unselfish love) and that her perception of the world is, if idealistic, traditional. When she speaks, however, it is in clichés and commonplaces: 'It will be summer and quiet in the fields. There will be stars and walking hand in hand'. To which Hinkemann brutally

retorts: 'It'll be autumn and the leaves falling. Cold stars –
and hate – and fist against fist' (S.P. 192). She lacks the
courage to live life on her own; her greatest fear is that
Hinkemann will not want her any more. She even invokes
the marriage service to make him stay with her:

> Don't leave me alone. I'm lost in the dark. I'll hurt
> myself. Oh, how it hurts, how it hurts. I'm so frightened
> to be alone. Think, Gene, think – all alone in the world.
> And nothing but wild beasts everywhere. No one to be
> good to you. Everyone tearing and biting and scratching.
> Don't leave me! Don't leave me! Whom God hath joined
> – I belong to you.   (S.P. 192)

The laughter which takes the form of a leitmotiv is used
ironically throughout the play. When Hinkemann kills the
blinded goldfinch out of pity he breaks into hysterical
laughter. He is obsessed by the idea that perhaps Grete is
laughing at him. When the customers in the pub learn that
'the strongest man in the world' is a eunuch they laugh; it is,
however, Grosshahn's callous lie that Grete had laughed at
Hinkemann which precipitates the tragedy. In the final
scene he explains to Grete why he is in despair:

> It's not because of my illness, not because I'm smashed
> up . . . But, you see, I walked along the street and there
> were no people – nothing but grinning faces, rows and
> rows of horrible grinning faces. . . . Living is only being
> hurt and wanting to go on. . . . *I won't go on*.
>   (S.P. 192)

Contrary to what the play may suggest, Toller never
completely abandoned Expressionism; he never gave up
his belief in the regeneration of man and the possibility of

achieving a new and better social order, although he recognised clearly the weaknesses of contemporary political systems. His letters, and especially his book, *Justiz. Erlebnisse*, are the best witnesses to this clear-sightedness. He is both an idealistic dreamer and a prescient political observer. In May 1923 he wrote to the actor Max Pallenberg:

> You may find out from *Hinkemann* which I am sending you ... the terrifying clear-sightedness with which I already sensed two years ago the disaster now developing in Germany. Even then I witnessed the signs of despair, of want and destitution, the breaking down of all ties. My *Wotan* is meant to help us find a way out of this intoxicated inertness. Whom do I attack with clubs? All those types who in my opinion have led us into the most deplorable mess, and who – if the people don't free themselves from their influence – will push them deeper and deeper into it. What has the German of a Goethe, Hölderlin or Büchner ... in common with the Teutonic nature of a Ruge, for example, or of a Theodor Fritsch or Adolf Hitler?   (T. 5/154)

Hinkemann is the only play which is little touched by this split attitude; in depicting the fate of *one* tragic individual Toller achieves for *Hinkemann* a degree of universality that transcends time and political institutions.

'Hoppla, wir leben!' ('Hoppla! Such is Life!')

Toller's first drama, *Die Wandlung*, produced in Martin's and Neppach's Expressionist style, established him among the leading playwrights of the 1920s; *Hoppla, wir leben!* which was presented on 3 September 1927, confirmed its director, Erwin Piscator, as Germany's leading director of proletarian theatre.

Born in 1893 in the German province of Hesse-Nassau, Piscator studied theatre history, among other subjects, at Munich University in 1913 and took up acting at the Munich Hoftheater in 1914. From 1915 to 1917 he served in the war. Like Toller, he became thoroughly disillusioned by his war experiences. After the war he became a dedicated Communist who considered the theatre an ideal platform for the political education of the proletariat. From 1920 he began to develop his political theatre which, at least until 1929, he identified with proletarian theatre; by then he had come to admit that the proletariat had not been capable of realising the importance of the theatre for their movement. But throughout his career he remained faithful to the credo with which he closes his book *Das politische Theater*:

> Our goal is to supersede bourgeois theater in terms of philosophy, dramatic theory, technique and staging. We are fighting for a restructured theater, and this must follow the lines of the social revolution.[5]

To realise his ideological aims, Piscator, who had worked at various Berlin theatres, especially at Die Volksbühne, came to the conclusion that none of the existing theatres satisfied his needs in terms of physical design; he began to envisage a *Totaltheater* (Total Theatre) incorporating new revolutionary concepts of space and design. Bauhaus director Walter Gropius designed for him such a theatre where the stage could be arranged in the following ways:

> There could be a proscenium stage for traditional plays (or a triple proscenium stage as in Van de Velde's

exhibition theatre at Cologne in 1912), or a circular arena stage which itself could revolve; or by revolving the whole half of the theatre containing this, seats and all, the circular stage could be brought round in front of the proscenium stage, to be used as a thrust stage or else covered in whole or in part with seats.[6]

This theatre was meant to involve the audience totally by employing all the media then available. Piscator was particularly fond of film, using it extensively in his productions as commentary on the play, or for the purpose of presenting simultaneous events. Gropius's plans were never realised because of the high construction and maintenance costs; however, from 1926 Piscator had the enthusiastic support of the great actress Tilla Durieux who persuaded her future husband, the tycoon Ludwig Katzenellenbogen, to finance Piscator's own first theatre, the Piscatorbühne at the Nollendorfplatz in Berlin, where he could best realise his ideas on staging. The theatre had a large revolving stage and was technically suitable for the installation of film- and slide-projectors, screens and loudspeakers. It also had the large seating capacity of eleven hundred. Piscator's immediate team consisted of designers and long-time friends, the famous painter George Grosz, John Heartfield (Helmut Herzfelde) and Traugott Müller; Edmund Meisel and Franz Osborn were the composers; among the actors who had agreed to perform in future productions were, of course, Tilla Durieux, and also Ernst Deutsch, Alexander Granach, Paul Graetz and Max Pallenberg.

Now that he had his own theatre, Piscator was able to realise a long-cherished plan to establish a Studio, a dramaturgical collective of authors, actors, directors, musicians and technical staff working together on selected plays; the Studio offered acting classes which included training in stylistics, foreign languages, theatre history, stage sets, costume and film-making. The Studio was perhaps the most interesting aspect of Piscator's attempt to realise his concept of the *Totaltheater*; he would later continue it in the form of the Dramatic Workshop which he established in New York in 1940 and which was attended by such actors as Tennessee Williams, Marlon Brando, Rod Steiger, Walter Matthau and Tony Curtis.

Piscator did not want to stage an already known play for the opening of his new theatre, the Piscatorbühne, but he had great difficulty in finding a suitable new political play. Patterson explains:

> . . . the Expressionist revolution in the theatre had been almost entirely an aesthetic revolution, and it had taken time for the public to cultivate a taste for Expressionist styles. Piscator's political theatre, however, derived from a sociological revolution, from the need to create a theatre reflecting the concerns of the proletariat. But even left-wing writers – like Toller – could not free themselves from their bourgeois individualism, and the proletariat had not yet brought forth its own writers.[7]

Piscator had originally intended to present a political revue dealing with the November Revolution of 1918. Wilhelm Herzog's commissioned play, *Rings um den Staatsanwalt* (*Round about the State's Attorney*) turned out, however, to be a 'lifeless, undramatic and dry account based on historical documents'. It was then that Piscator turned to Toller, who in the spring of 1927 had sent him a sketch of *Hoppla, wir leben!* Piscator liked the basic idea of a play about a 'revolutionary's clash with the world of 1927 after having spent eight years in a mental institution'.

The plot of the play is simple. The prologue introduces and defines the key characters: Karl Thomas, Eva Berg, Wilhelm Kilman, Frau Meller and Albert Kroll, all revolutionaries awaiting execution. The death sentence is changed to a sentence of imprisonment except for Kilman who is freed and for Karl Thomas who is sent to an asylum because he had gone mad while waiting to be executed.

The following five acts depict Karl Thomas's struggle to resume a normal life after eight years in the mental hospital. But times have changed and no one wants to hear about the Revolution and its aims any more. Kilman, whom Karl Thomas thought dead, has become a Minister of the Republic, associated with shady bankers, who claims he can better the condition of the proletariat by working within the system; Eva Berg, whom Thomas loves, has become a dedicated political young woman out to improve the working conditions of female factory workers; she has no time for Thomas's 'sentimental' feelings. Albert Kroll, formerly an idealist revolutionary, has become a worker who fights corruption in government and tries to organise and educate the proletariat; Frau Meller is still a determined fighter for the rights of her class. When Thomas fails to find a job in his profession as a typesetter, he becomes a kitchen hand in the Grand Hotel. There he meets Kilman again and decides to kill him because he has betrayed the Revolution. By a twist of fate Kilman is shot by a small-fry anti-semitic anarchist just at the moment when Thomas has given up his plan. He finds himself back in prison together with his friends. Unable to stand this 'madhouse of a world' any longer and afraid to endure again the dreadful experience of waiting for his execution, he hangs himself just before he is found innocent. In the final, bitterly ironic close, Count Lande, who had hired Kilman's assassin, unveils a statue to Kilman.

Hoppla, wir leben! is among the best plays of *aktuelles Theater* (actual or political theatre) written in the 1920s in Germany, offering a satirical and pessimistic picture of society in the Weimar Republic. Toller conveys powerfully the spectrum of political and industrial life dominated principally by a lust for power; once again he dramatises the exploitation of ordinary people and their futile struggle against the economic apparatus which enslaves them. Already in *Hinkemann* Toller had begun to incorporate scenes depicting actual events of the 1920s but he used them only as background material. In *Hoppla, wir leben!* Toller's primary concern is to depict the corrupt institutions of the Weimar Republic, as the scenes that take place in the polling station and the Grand Hotel demonstrate. Karl Thomas becomes the vehicle which Toller uses in a variety of situations to describe what was wrong with society and why, exactly in the way Erich Kästner uses the figure of Fabian in his novel *Fabian* (1932).

Karl Thomas is a good illustration of how Toller's earlier idealism has been tempered by time and experience. Thomas is a dreamer unwilling and unable to confront reality. When he is forced to do so, he prefers death by suicide. In contrast to Hinkemann who still arouses compassion and understanding in his friends, Karl Thomas's ideas about personal happiness and political action are greeted with disdain. Since *Masse Mensch* Toller had juxtaposed dialectically other and different ideas to those of his protagonists. However, he had never gone as far as in *Hoppla, wir leben!* where Thomas's ideals are bluntly rejected, even ridiculed. His proposal, for example, to Eva Berg to escape with him into a 'saner' world is scorned by her:

You're disgusted with politics? Do you imagine you

could break away from them? Do you imagine that a southern sun, palm trees, elephants, coloured clothes, would make you forget the way mankind really lives? The paradise you dream about does not exist.

(S.P. 225–6)

Similarly, his political opinions are rejected by his friend Kroll:

KARL THOMAS: What does the election matter to me? Show me your faith, the old faith which was to have moved mountains.

ALBERT KROLL: You mean, I no longer have it? Do you want me to tell you how often we've wanted to throw off the cursed yoke? Do you want to name the old comrades who were murdered, locked up, and hunted?

KARL THOMAS: Only faith matters.

ALBERT KROLL: We want no blessedness in heaven. One must learn to see straight and yet not allow oneself to be downtrodden.

(S.P. 236)

When Thomas accuses his fellow workers of being cowards, Kroll retorts: 'You seem to expect the world to be a sort of eternal firework display got up for your benefit, with rockets and catherine-wheels and battle-cries. It's you who're the coward, not I' (S.P. 237). Karl Thomas believes that by killing the corrupt Kilman he can bring about political renovation but he is brought to realise that Kilman's death would be absolutely useless because the Minister would be replaced by others exactly like him. When Kilman is shot Thomas is shocked to learn that the assassin mistakenly believed Kilman to be a Bolshevik and a revolutionary who could sell out the country to the Jews.

The scene immediately following this revelation is in its atmosphere quite similar to the snow scene in Kaiser's *Von morgens bis mitternachts*. In style it is the most Expressionist in the play. In both cases the protagonists are forced to recognise that they have been fundamentally wrong in their assumptions; now they must come to terms with their new *Weltbild* (concept of the World). Once more Thomas is sent to the mental hospital for observation, but by now he recognises that the psychiatrist, Lüdin, and the politicians and their military agents are far more dangerous to mankind than the mental cases in their cells. He is sent back to prison by Lüdin who sees in Thomas 'the arch-enemy of all civilisation' who must be 'sterilised, eliminated', because he has now passed through a period of education in his relationship with Kilman, Kroll and Eva Berg.

After the fiasco with Herzog's play, Piscator collaborated closely with his new author in order to ensure that the final product would accord with his ideas about political drama. They began work together at the end of June 1927, and continued up to the premiere. It turned out to be a strained collaboration because Piscator took the liberty of adding and rewriting scenes without the knowledge of Toller who usually discovered such changes at rehearsals and was understandably annoyed. Both men differed widely about the character of Karl Thomas (Piscator disliked Toller's heroes because of their 'mixed' character). In *Das politische Theater* he writes:

> But the documentary material was overlaid with poetic lyricism, as was always the case in Toller's work. All our efforts in the subsequent course of the work were directed towards providing the play with a realistic substructure. . . . Even at the very first reading in my old house in Oranienstrasse, the figure of the 'hero', Karl

Thomas, came under heated attack. His character was accused of being too passive and ill-defined. Toller tends to impose the burden of his own feelings on such characters, and these are subject to the restless fluctuations which are typical of artists, particularly if they have been through as much and suffered as much as Toller.[8]

Piscator's conception of Thomas's character finally prevailed over Toller's when Piscator made the actor Granach 'play the hero as a solid, walrus-moustached proletarian, not at all the "little son of a bourgeois" specified in the prologue'.[9]

They disagreed especially about the conclusion of the play; Piscator's version (which also appears in the published version of 1927) has Karl Thomas commit suicide after his arrest. Toller's original version was in the form of a four-act play with Karl Thomas finally returning voluntarily to the mental hospital because he thinks he cannot cope with the world of 1927 any more. However, after a conversation with the doctor he discovers that 'there are two kinds of dangerous madmen, the ones locked away in their isolation cells and the others who as politicians and military rage against humankind' (T. 1/147). Thus enlightened he wants to join his old friends in their daily struggle but is kept in the asylum because for the doctor he now represents a true enemy of the state. This scene is a particularly cynical one, fitting the message of the play better than the ending written for Piscator. On the other hand, Karl Thomas's death in that eerie last scene where the prisoners communicate through knocking on the cell walls and where the knocking rises into a final thunder followed by an abrupt silence is dramatically so effective, and also more in line with Thomas's character, that it was adopted (with one exception) in all other productions of the play following the Piscator one. Piscator's prompt book reveals that he had even tampered with this ending, adding a few lines in order to underline the political message. Toller's play ended with Eva Berg's statement: 'He makes no sign'. Piscator added:

RAND (*Cries out*): Hanged!!!
MELLER: Is that true?
KROLL: How could he do this, this is no way for revolutionaries to die.
EVA: The world has broken him down.
MELLER: Damned world! We must change it.

(T. 3/326)

In *Hoppla, wir leben!* Toller introduced a number of film sequences, that is the prologue and three interludes. Toller might have done so at the suggestion of Piscator who was eager to incorporate this medium in the forthcoming production; however, Toller himself was fascinated by modern stage techniques, and the dream episodes in his earlier plays can be considered as forerunners of the filmstrips. Piscator, however, did not always follow Toller's suggestion on what to present on these films; where Toller referred to world politics, Piscator showed more immediately relevant events, but the film shown during the prologue in particular (and also the sequence before scene two of Act One) turned the prologue indeed into a dreamlike episode, more characteristic of Toller than of Piscator. Patterson, whose step-by-step description of this Piscator production makes fascinating reading, is puzzled by Piscator's move away from his otherwise realistic directing approach:

Clearly, the film here did not possess any objective or

documentary function, but was used simply to create atmosphere to enclose the prisoners from in front and from behind with images of menace. In a note in the prompt-book Piscator emphasised the subject nature of these film sequences in a curiously Expressionist manner: 'The actor reacts to the film images as though he were seeing them. They become *his* hallucinations, *his* terror; the events on film describe *his* imagination.'[10]

Although Toller had not written a *danse macabre* scene – so cherished by him in his earlier plays – Mary Wigman, a pupil of Rudolf von Laban, and the choreographer of *Hoppla, wir leben!*, ingeniously and appropriately created one immediately after scene four of Act Four where Karl Thomas is confronted again by the mad psychiatrist, Lüdin, who wants to prove to him that the world is normal:

Before the final act Mary Wigman's female dancers performed a Charleston. They were costumed as skeletons, and danced in ultra-violet light which gave a phosphorescent effect to their 'bones' and skull-like make-up. Besides filling an awkward gap in an entertaining manner, a Charleston performed by skeletons was a powerful comment by Piscator on the precarious nature of German prosperity in 1927: society was dancing in a charnel house.[11]

This same idea is expressed in Walter Mehring's chanson, 'Hopla, wir leben!' written for the Piscator production with music by Edmund Meisel; it was sung by Käte Kühl as introduction to the Grand Hotel scenes:

In this hotel called earth
The *Crème* of society are the guests –

They carry with little concern
 Life's heavy burden!
 The enemies are beat –
 Give the cripple over there a penny
 We are so short ourselves!
 The ministers, the thinkers and poets:
 They are the same old faces!
 It's exactly as before the war –
 Before the next war, I mean –
 The Charleston is the battlesong:
 Hopla! *they* live!   (T. 3/334)

Toller's stage directions for the play indicate that 'all
scenes of the play can be played on a tiered scaffold which
would make scene changes unnecessary'. His scheme for
the Grand Hotel became the set of the whole play (T.
3/78). Stage designer Traugott Müller together with Otto
Richter created an *Etagenbühne* (tiered structure) which

Schema:

87	88	89	W/C	90	91	92	93	94	95	96 offen	97	98
26	27	28	29	30	31	32	33	34	W/C	35	36	37

Grand Hotel / Radiostation

Separé / Dienstbotenzimmer und Office / Vestibül / Klubraum / Schreibzimmer provided Piscator with the possibility of simultaneous staging which 'could be used to order sequences in temporal and spatial terms instead of relying on dialogue to move the action'.[12]

Having learned from his failure in attempting to stage scenes simultaneously in his 1926 production of Schiller's *Die Räuber* at the Berlin Volksbühne, Piscator this time contented himself with the *illusion* of simultaneous staging in that he used lighting and black-outs to separate the scenes staged on the tiered structure. This mobile scaffold with its complex apparatus was a novelty in stage design; it was so self-contained that it was, in fact, a stage within a stage. The front of the structure was covered by a gauze for film or slide projections, the backcloth had the same screen function. Using the film/slide medium Piscator achieved simultaneity through the technique of overlaying. In fact, technology became more important for *Hoppla, wir leben!* than the actors' interpretation; Piscator tended to treat his actors as automata. His main flaw was, however, that he had a compulsion to experiment and constantly to introduce new ideas or changes which turned production preparations often enough into sheer pandemonium that sometimes even carried over into opening night. One critic sums up the problems of the Piscator productions:

Not only was Piscator notorious for his autocratic alterations of texts but he constantly overreached himself in his efforts to create contemporary theatrical forms with insufficient materials, and the elements he substituted for the literary qualities of a play were clumsy and frequently malfunctioned. The weight of the acting structure for *Hoppla!* made it difficult to move around the stage. Even with the lavish application of soap, graphite and lubricating oil the treadmills that he had invented for *Schweik* tended to drown the actors' voices. The global construct for *Rasputin* had fallen apart in one performance, ... *The Merchant of Berlin* was in one sense the culmination of his efforts; but looked at in another light it was a technological disaster.[13]

Hoppla, wir leben! was to be premiered simultaneously on 1 September in Hamburg at the Kammerspiele, director Hanns Lotz, and in Berlin, but while the Hamburg premiere took place as scheduled Piscator had to postpone the Berlin premiere to 3 September because of technical difficulties:

> After the many weeks of work my only feeling was: nothing can be changed now. The work had been done, even if it was a bit rough in many places and had not been given all the finishing touches. Even on the opening night when the first curtain was timed at 7:00 P.M., I came across Gasbarra and Guttmann at 7:45 in a basement room editing parts of the film clips which were to run upstairs at 8:00 P.M. Even during the performance I was issuing new instructions, and during the intermission I altered the lighting for a few of the scenes. At 6:45 when the public were already on their way to their seats we were still trying out the film code messages for the finale.

The evening, despite its length (four hours instead of two), turned out to be a great success and the premiere ended in a way even Piscator had not dreamt of:

> When the curtain fell . . . the young proletarians struck up the 'Internationale' and we all rose and sang it to the end. To the consternation of the *beau monde*, who had known that they were paying up to 100 marks for a seat

1. Ernst Toller in 1927.

Georg Kaiser

2. Georg Kaiser in 1922.

3. Toller's *Transfiguration* produced in 1919 by Karlheinz Martin and Robert Neppach at the Tribüne Theatre, Berlin.

4. Kaiser's *From Morning to Midnight* produced by Viktor Barnowsky in 1921 in Berlin. *The snow field* sketch by César Klein.

KAISER : HÖLLE WEG ERDE   CÉSAR KLEIN

5. Kaiser's *Hell, Way, Earth* produced by Viktor Barnowsky at the Lessing
Theatre, Berlin, in 1920. Sketch by César Klein.

6. Mary Dietrich in Toller's *Masses and Man* produced by Jürgen Fehling at the Berlin Volksbühne in 1921.

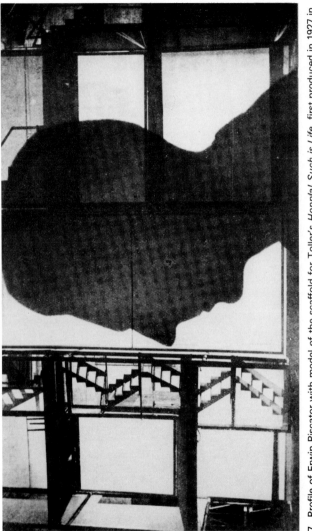

7. Profile of Erwin Piscator with model of the scaffold for Toller's *Hoppla! Such is Life*, first produced in 1927 in Berlin.

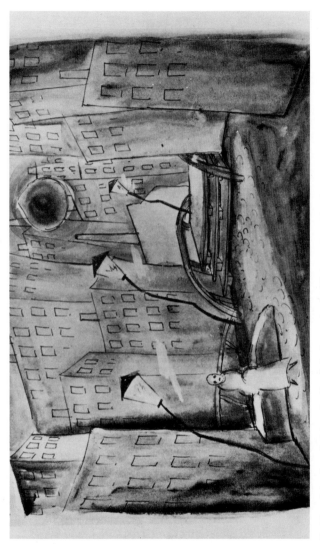

8. Sketch by Otto Reigbert for Brecht's *Drums in the Night* produced by Otto Falckenburg in 1922.

9. Paul Shelving's design of the English production of Kaiser's *Gas*, in 1923 at the Repertory Theatre, Birmingham.

in the 'Communist provocateur's theater,' but had never imagined that the evening could end with a political demonstration.[14]

Apart from Nazi-oriented reviews which condemned *Hoppla, wir leben!* for political reasons, the general press acclaimed the production. Its technical effects, especially the use of film and sound effects, made an overwhelming impression; particularly impressive was the scene at the Radio Station of the Grand Hotel where Karl Thomas (and the audience) hear the news from all over the world, including the heart-beat of an airline passenger:

OPERATOR: Six-day race in Milan. . . . Now I'll hear something interesting. The first passenger aeroplane from New York–Paris announced that a passenger has been overcome by a heart attack. He wants to connect up with heart specialist. Doctor's advice wanted. Now you hear the heart-beat of the patient.
(*On the* LOUDSPEAKER *one hears the beating of a heart. On the screen, aeroplane over the ocean. The patient.*)
(S.P. 248)

The performance of the actors Granach and Graetz (in the comic role of Pickel), and Käte Kühl's interpretation of Mehring's song were highly praised.

Piscator's ingenious and lavish staging tended to over-shadow Toller's play. Critics were inclined to argue that Piscator's direction had improved a somewhat mediocre play. But *Hoppla, wir leben!* was performed with great success in places other than Berlin and under different directors. It is a very good play in its own right and its text is strong enough to refute the charge that it can be rescued only by a brilliant stage director.

'Pastor Hall'

With *Hoppla, wir leben!* Toller's fame as a playwright reached its climax; none of his future works display the vitality and originality of this and the others written in Niederschönenfeld. His fame also suffered because the Nazi authorities deliberately ignored his work, and because the public's interest in Expressionist drama and *aktuelles Theater* had waned. His play *Bourgeois bleibt Bourgeois* was a total failure despite its carefully planned 1929 production – no script is known to exist. *Wunder in Amerika* which was premiered on 17 October 1931 in Mannheim was no more successful. The best play Toller wrote in this period was *Feuer aus den Kesseln*, an historical drama depicting the revolt of the German Navy in 1917 and the ensuing trial of some of the crew. Although it earned the highest critical acclaim when it was premiered on 31 August 1930 at the Theater am Schiffbauerdamm in Berlin, it failed to attract wide public support. Wrote theatre manager, Ernst Josef Aufricht: 'The realistic *Zeittheater* of the Twenties was dead'.

The murder of Erich Mühsam in the concentration camp of Oranienburg in 1934, and the accounts of the cruel treatment of prisoners in German concentration camps in general which Toller learned from an escapee, Willi Bredel, in the same year, suggested the theme for his last play, *Pastor Hall*. He began it in 1938 and finished it just a few months before his death. Rejected for performance by the Dramatists Play Service in New York, it was, however, published in 1939 in the United States as well as in England. In 1940 it was made into a film with Wilfried Lawson in the leading role.[15] When shown in the States the film was preceded by a prologue spoken by Eleanor

Roosevelt. Although having misgivings about 'the small budget production', the press hailed the film as being thus far the best documentation of the rampant barbarism in Hitler's Germany. An attempt was made to show the film in Mexico (under the title *The Martyr*) but it was withdrawn after a few days because of bomb threats from a group of Nazi supporters.

In Germany *Pastor Hall* received its premiere only after the War; in the Deutsches Theater, Berlin, on 24 January 1947. The director was Thomas Engel, the designer Heinrich Goertz. It ran for thirty-three performances and the reception, as always in Toller's case, was mixed. Critics found the characters to be weak; the clergy felt offended by Toller's treatment of Pastor Hall; politically minded critics (generally right-wing) felt that the play would appeal primarily to an 'anti-fascist' audience. The emotional tone of most contemporary reviews is probably due to the fact that it was too soon, in 1947, to confront Germans so bluntly with their immediate past. Carl Zuckmayer's play *Des Teufels General* (*The Devil's General*), which was premiered in the same year as *Pastor Hall*, was much more warmly received, perhaps because the central character, the General, is portrayed as a 'good' German who, while he disliked the Hitler regime, remained in the Luftwaffe out of a love of flying. Neither Zuckmayer nor most of his audience realised that a character like General Harras is, in fact, dangerous because he never comes to realise the degree of his complicity with Nazism; the success of the play was based on a misconception of the protagonist's role.

Pastor Hall is about a German priest who is brought to a true understanding of his character and thereby discovers it to be his duty openly to oppose the Nazis. The antagonist is Fritz Gerte, a former clerk, a good-for-nothing, now a member of the *Totenkopf SS* (Death Head SS). Gerte, who wishes to marry Hall's daughter, Christine, attempts to blackmail the Halls because they have violated Nazi currency laws. When he refuses to co-operate with Gerte, Hall is imprisoned in a concentration camp. Act Two takes place in the camp where Hall witnesses scenes of torture. Confident in his own strength he refuses his wife's plea that he sign a paper renouncing his activities against the Nazis. However, when he himself is sentenced to be tortured he cannot face it and escapes with the aid of a young SS officer, a former pupil who is himself shot by the prison guards. In the final act Hall determines that it is his duty to speak out publicly against Nazi tyranny. The play ends with the pastor, accompanied by his family and an old friend, General Grotjahn, making his way to the church to preach his sermon as a military column approaches.

Pastor Hall is a final treatment of the transformation theme of *Die Wandlung* and *Masse Mensch* within the traditional framework of a three-act play. Because the play is based on the political reality of Nazi Germany, Toller modifies considerably the way in which the transformation of Pastor Hall is effected. In *Die Wandlung* and in *Masse Mensch* the protagonists undergo a transformation that relates primarily to their ideology: the transformation does not grow out of a change or development in character. Pastor Hall, on the other hand, undergoes a transformation in which both his character and his ideas are radically modified. At the beginning of the play he is a self-righteous preacher who puts principle before human compassion. When his wife begs him to delay their daughter's marriage to save them all from prison, he declares: 'No, Ida, here human consideration ends – even to you, my wife. I cannot betray the principles of humanity because some fanatic, gorged with power, tries to blackmail me.' His wife retorts bitterly: 'During these last years you have never even considered to what hell you might be leaving your child and your wife – only yourself, yourself, yourself. If that's Christianity, I'd rather be a pagan.'[16] Here again is a familiar Toller theme – the conflict between principle grounded on abstract values and values based on human considerations and the necessity to survive.

The conflict is further dramatised in the prison scenes of Act Two and notably in a seminal exchange with the Communist, Peter Hofer. Hall voices the pacifism and idealism of Toller's early protagonists; Hofer voices a realism more akin to that of Albert Kroll, the dedicated union organiser of *Hoppla, wir leben!*

FRIEDRICH HALL: . . . Today I believe only in the way of understanding and of love. There's no question on earth which can't be settled without force, however complicated and entangled it is.

PETER HOFER: It takes two to arrive at a solution without force, Herr Pastor. It isn't we who invite force, it's the others. Shall I be robbed of my right and say thank you very much? I'd rather die.

FRIEDRICH HALL: The courage to die has become cheap, so cheap that I often ask myself whether it isn't a flight from life.[17]

But when Hall is put to the test he breaks, unlike the Woman in *Masse Mensch*. She refused to escape because it would mean the death of the guard. Because of his fear of torture the pastor escapes and causes the death of the young SS guard. 'I brought the punishment on myself,' the pastor confesses, 'because I was proud and wanted to show how strong I was . . .' But now, as he tells his wife, he is 'a man who's broken down, and who needs you, needs your

protection, your warmth, your kind, foolish heart'.[18] Again,
like Kaiser in *Die Bürger von Calais*, Toller insists on the
necessity for the 'Wandlung' to be authentic. The General
and Hall's family beg him to run away but he refuses. In *Die
Wandlung* Toller, idealistically and naively, had Friedrich's
message change people and society for the better; with
greater realism, however, Toller has Pastor Hall understand that he has no power over Nazis like Gerte. He has no
illusions now that he can change the prevalent ideology; it
can only be resisted. Significantly his certain death is not
sought out of cheap courage nor is it suicidal: it is, rather, an
act of affirmation and sacrifice that quite clearly implies an
ultimate vindication:

> FRIEDRICH HALL (*very softly*): I will live. It will be like a
> fire that no might can put out, the meek will tell the
> meek and they'll become brave again. One man will
> tell another that the anti-Christ rules, the destroyer,
> the enemy of mankind – and they will find strength and
> follow my example.[19]

The tolling of the church bell at the play's close is clearly
meant to suggest Hall's martyrdom but it also carries Hall's
words throughout a land dominated by the final sounds of
the marching Nazis.

Pastor Hall is not a good play. Too many of the *dramatis
personae* are stereotypes (Gerte the 'bad' Nazi, Grotjahn
the 'good' German officer), and the play lacks the vitality of
the earlier works perhaps because Toller was too close to
his material (he even introduces a passage recounting the
death in a concentration camp of his friend, Erich
Mühsam). But it is to be valued for showing Toller's deep
and enduring belief in the possibility of the regeneration of
social values and of human society. In this he remained true

to the Expressionist ideals which proclaimed the imminence of a New Man. Pastor Hall's final speech of affirmation and hope returns full circle to the transfiguration motif of Toller's first play and to its final triumphant chorus:

> Brothers, stretch out your tortured hands
> With cries of radiant, ringing joy!
> Stride freely through our liberated land
> With cries of Revolution, Revolution!

5

Georg Kaiser: Life and Art

'I live for Georg Kaiser.' *G. Kaiser*

It is a phenomenon of literature that it sometimes produces twin artists who dominate their period as, for example, Lope de Vega and Calderón in Spain, Racine and Corneille in France, Goethe and Schiller in Germany. In German Expressionist drama Toller and Kaiser tower over their contemporaries and, although the movement had been prepared by others, it was they who established drama firmly within the Expressionist movement.

Georg Kaiser was Germany's most successful and widely performed dramatist until 1933, when his works were forbidden by the Nazis. By that time, Kaiser had written more than fifty plays, forty-five of which had been performed. Although he continued writing until his death (nineteen more plays, numerous short stories and filmscripts, two complete novels, one fragment and a number of essays) his public career was ruined. Of the plays written after 1933, only seven were performed during his lifetime and for very short periods only. When he died in 1945 in Swiss exile, he had only a few friends with him; his wife, who had stayed behind in Germany, heard of his death on the radio.

Although Kaiser is Germany's most prolific playwright, he wrote little about his personal life, and what autobiographical information we possess must be accepted cautiously since he purposely distorted or falsified facts out of an obsessive wish to preserve his privacy. He was born on 25 November 1878 in Magdeburg, the fifth of six sons. His father was a prosperous chief insurance agent; his mother, sixteen years younger than her husband, was apparently a vivacious but high-strung person. Kaiser said of her that she 'existed only in extremes; she was either swimming in tears or ecstatically happy'.[1] Kaiser seemed to have been a nervous child with a tendency to stand out from the crowd. He adored soccer and bicycling but school bored him because of the pedantry of his teachers. Other German authors like Thomas Mann, Kafka, Wedekind and Toller have written bitterly about their 'education'; Heinrich Mann's novel *Professor Unrat* (*Professor Filth*), which became world famous when made into the film *Der blaue Engel* (*The Blue Angel*), is one of the most cynical satires on the German school system of the second half of the nineteenth century. Kaiser's plays *Der Fall des Schülers Vehgesack* (*Pupil Vehgesack's Case*), 1901–2, and *Rektor Kleist*, 1903, draw upon his experiences in school.

He early developed an avid interest in reading and until the end of his life read an incredible number of newspapers and books, modern authors as well as the classics. His favoured author was, and would remain, Plato. Since his father was about to retire and did not then have the means to put a fourth son through a costly education, Kaiser, who had no inclination for an academic career, became an apprentice in a bookshop but left it after a few weeks. He entered an import-export business for coffee but in 1898, after three years, he left Magdeburg for Buenos Aires where he found work with a branch of the Berlin General Electric Company. Illness forced him to return home in 1901. Throughout his life Kaiser maintained that he had contracted malaria in Argentina and that it was responsible for his recurring attacks of ill-health. In Magdeburg his state of health grew worse; he was plagued by insomnia, restlessness and nervous convulsions. He finally underwent treatment with the Berlin neurologist-psychiatrist, Dr Laehr, who in a 1902 medical statement wrote of Kaiser:

> All these nervous and psychic disorders are nothing else but psycho-pathetic and hysterical reactions against his milieu which deep down bothered Kaiser . . . He feels the urgent need to manifest without restriction his talent which he has recognised for a long time and of which he thinks highly; he really longs and strives for the triumph – which he claims to scorn, 'to publish from my [Kaiser's] immortal works'.[2]

Dr Laehr had analysed Kaiser quite correctly. In 1919, for example, Kaiser writes to the theatre director, Otto Liebscher, about *Der gerettete Alkibiades* (*Alkibiades Saved*) that no other writer could produce anything of this kind 'in the next 323 years, three months, one week, 4 days, etc'.[3] And in 1943 he states in a letter to his wife about *Das Floss der Medusa* (*The Raft of the Medusa*): 'It will become a triumph of dramatic art and stage-craft in Germany. How proud this country can be that this unique work was written in German. Who is there at this time to master it better than I? There is nobody, far and wide, who equals me.'[4]

From 1901 until 1905 Kaiser felt too ill to practise any profession and these years of apparent inactivity were, in reality, a period of intellectual germination: 'However, in those five years, where the world had disappeared for me, where I sat almost motionless at the window of my room there I discovered a world which did not exist, the more real world of literature' (K. 4/605).

In 1908 he married Margarethe Habenicht, and because of her dowry was able for the first time in his life to lead the existence he had always dreamed of. But the money was soon used up and from then on Kaiser was constantly in debt despite the high income he received from the productions and publications of his works. Believing idiosyncratically that an artist of his rank was entitled to live extravagantly, he rented the most expensive villas, stayed only in first-class hotels, and continued this style of living even during the years of exile when he was unable to pay his bills. His irresponsibility in money matters led to a notorious trial and his imprisonment. In order to cover some of his enormous debts (more than 300,000 marks) and to provide for his family – a third child had just been born – Kaiser had pawned and sold furnishings and valuables from an apartment and a villa which he was renting near Munich. On 13 October 1920, he was arrested in Berlin and taken to Munich where he was imprisoned, while his wife and children were put in the poorhouse.

Kaiser, by then Germany's most famous playwright, apart from Gerhart Hauptmann, was outraged by his treatment in prison, as were many of his friends. The trial, on 15 February 1921, became a sensation and quickly developed political overtones because of his friendship with Gustav Landauer and the 'traitor' Ernst Toller (Kaiser was accused of being a Communist). He was given a one-year sentence but was released from prison in April

1921. His defence speech is among the most revealing and egotistic statements he ever made about his art:

> I hold myself to be an extravagantly exceptional case. The law does not apply to me. . . . He who has created much is *a priori* exempt from punishment. The obligation I have towards myself is higher than my obligation to the law. . . . The idea that everybody is equal before the law is nonsensical. I am not everybody. I am great, therefore I am permitted to break the law. Even though I might be considered childish, I must declare that I am unspeakably great! My arrest is not only a personal disaster, it is a national disaster. The flags should have been set at half-mast. (K. 4/562)

Kaiser began writing at the early age of seventeen. His first plays were dramatic 'exercises' rather than full-length dramas, and predictably they display the influence of various styles. 1911 marks the beginning of the regular publication of his works; by then Kaiser had already written twenty-one plays. Two plays in this first period are particularly interesting. The comedy *Die jüdische Witwe* (*The Jewish Widow*), 1904, based on the biblical study of Judith and Holofernes, is a psychological study of the battle of the sexes from which Judith emerges as by far the stronger and more powerful; it was the first Kaiser play to be published (1911). The second, *König Hahnrei* (*King Cuckold*), 1910, is another psychological drama; it depicts the legend of Tristan and Isolt from an unusual angle in that its protagonist is the tragic figure of King Mark, who cannot bring himself to accept his wife's adultery because then his suffering would be unbearable. This work already displays many features of Kaiser's Expressionist style.

Kaiser's second and Expressionist period commences

with the play *Von morgens bis mitternachts (From Morning to Midnight)*, 1912. Though brief (*Gats*, written in 1924, marks its end), this is the most important period of his career. His next play *Die Bürger von Calais* (*The Burghers of Calais*) was premiered on 29 January 1917 at the Neues Theater in Frankfurt, directed by Arthur Hellmer. The production marked the beginning of Kaiser's comet-like rise and created so-called Frankfurt Expressionism. Equally successful was the premiere of *Von morgens bis mitternachts* in the Munich Kammerspiele on 28 April 1917. Among the audience were Bertolt Brecht and Rainer Maria Rilke, who was so impressed that he saw the play three times. Although *Von morgens bis mitternachts* and *Die Bürger von Calais* were Kaiser's first attempts in Expressionist drama, they are classic examples of this genre. The former is a *Stationendrama*; the latter develops Kaiser's most optimistic vision of the New Man. Both were highly influential on other Expressionists, including Toller. In 1919 Kaiser met and befriended Toller, whose play *Die Wandlung* was published with Kaiser's support. The attraction between these two men was a peculiar one since they were totally opposite in character, looks and aims. Hermann Kesten describes Toller as a 'beautiful man with great charisma who knew how to charm people', while he remembers Kaiser as a sober, down-to-earth person who would have passed for an average citizen 'had he not had the eyes of a madman'. In contrast to Toller, Kaiser did not engage in politics; he was sympathetic to the left not out of conviction but because of his opposition to the reactionary bourgeoisie.

Brecht, who was then a theatre critic in Augsburg, reviewed Kaiser's play *Gas* in 1919; he was fascinated with this new form of drama, and his first three plays are deeply indebted to Kaiser's Expressionist style. The *Stationen-*

technik greatly influenced him in formulating his theory of Epic theatre. Although he called Kaiser his adopted father, he later condemned the Expressionists' idealistic belief in the power of human love as embarrassingly unrealistic and would have preferred a more realistic political engagement. He further criticised the Expressionist language which, he felt, fluctuated between *Telegrammstil* (telegraph style) and *Pathos* (elevated style). The *Telegrammstil* came dangerously close to journalistic jargon while the *Pathos* used, for example, in *Die Wandlung* and *Die Bürger von Calais*, he argued, 'reveals nothing much' on close examination. He accused Kaiser in particular of yelling rather than speaking. Despite his criticism, Brecht recognised the importance of Kaiser's role in the development of contemporary drama and film. Fritz Lang's famous film *Metropolis*, for example, is Kaiserian in many aspects.

After the success of *Die Bürger von Calais* and *Von morgens bis mitternachts*, Kaiser became feverishly productive; he wrote at such speed that some of his publishers and directors expressed doubts about the authorship of his plays. 'He doesn't take time to learn how to write', Brecht complained, 'because he is too busy writing plays!' He also actively promoted them and assisted at rehearsals despite his claims that he never saw his own plays, and that he did not write with the public in mind. 'It always astonished me that the plays I wrote were stageable. Never did I even peer with one eye on the stage while working on the manuscript ... creation does not permit a public' (K. 4.552). Kaiser even directed one of his own plays, *Der Brand im Opernhaus* (*The Fire in the Opera House*), 1917–18, in the Berlin Kleines Schauspielhaus. Max Reinhardt, who was not interested in Expressionist drama and staged only a few such plays, agreed to let Kaiser direct the play, which was premiered on 26 November 1918.

Kaiser continued in the Expressionist genre, exploring the idea of a regeneration of mankind from different angles and in different settings, as Toller did in his first three plays. His *Hölle Weg Erde* (*Hell Way Earth*), 1918–19, another *Stationendrama*, depicts the transformation motif in a positive way. The trilogy, *Die Koralle* (*The Coral*), 1916–17, *Gas I*, 1917–18, and *Gas II*, 1918–19, begins idealistically with the message that a better Man will be born but as it develops it turns into Kaiser's most pessimistic statement about the future of mankind. In their prophetic vision of a society doomed to destruction they utter as powerful an anti-Utopia statement as any drama of the twentieth century.

The years of the 1920s were beyond doubt Kaiser's happiest; he now lived with his family in Grünheide near Berlin where he had also rented an apartment which became the meeting place of a group of artists, among them Brecht, Yvan Goll and his wife Claire; there the fabulous Lotte Lenya met the composer Kurt Weill, whom she would later marry. Kaiser also met a number of stage directors, among them Karlheinz Martin whose first Expressionist film was based on Kaiser's play *Von morgens bis mitternachts*. Kaiser even planned on acquiring the Theater am Schiffbauerdamm for his own plays. The actor Eugen Klöpfer was to become its director with the Expressionist painter, Max Pechstein, as designer. (The plan fell through for lack of finances.) He travelled extensively, constantly promoting his works; he was now established as leading author of the publishing house Die Schmiede, and he actively furthered the careers of many young writers.[5] In 1926 he was elected a member of the Prussian Arts Academy.

Some critics argue that Kaiser's drama is too intellectualised. Bernhard Diebold, for example, characterised him as a *Denkspieler* (a manipulator of ideas), arguing that his plays lack warmth and feeling because they are unrelated to personal experiences. But this is a misconception. When Kaiser fell in love with the young actress, Blanche Dergan, he wrote for her the play *Die Flucht nach Venedig* (*The Flight to Venice*) in 1922, which depicts a period in the love relationship between Alfred de Musset and George Sand. In a letter to Blanche Dergan he states how much their relationship had stimulated this work:

> This work has emerged from the experience with you: there cannot be a deeper basis for a human relationship. Experience which does not eventually result in creative work is not worthwhile and has not ripened. The poetic work – grown out of experience – becomes a document of the greatness of love – and of intimacy like no other document. . . . My love for you, Blanche Sand, will have Alfred de Musset find words about love which have never yet been said. Musset will be destroyed by it – I want to live with you in the greater realm of love.[6]

In approximately 1919, Kaiser met Maria von Mühlfeld (Mary Fischel) – his future mistress – and their relationship lasted until his death. The theme of his first novel *Es ist genug* (*It is Enough*), 1930–1, is based on his relationship with Maria von Mühlfeld and their daughter, Olivia, born in 1927. Until November 1945 Margarethe Kaiser had no knowledge about this affair.

From 1923 on Kaiser wrote a number of comedies for he quickly recognised that at a time of economic and political upheaval audiences preferred lighter entertainment to the heavier fare of Expressionist drama. Already cinemas and cabarets had sprung up, among them the famous Berlin Wintergarten. His witty play *Kolportage* (*Colportage*),

1923–4, was premiered on 23 March 1924 in Berlin at the Lessing Theater and also in Frankfurt at the Neues Theater. In 1925–6 Kaiser and Weill collaborated on *Zweimal Oliver* (*Twice Oliver*), a play in three parts; it is based on an earlier one-act Kaiser play and tells the story of a stage hero who continues to act out his roles in reality. It was premiered on 15 April 1926 in the Dresden Schauspielhaus and in the same year played in eight more German theatres.

Another collaboration between Kaiser and Weill resulted in an *opera buffa*: *Der Zar lässt sich photographieren* (*The Tzar has his Picture Taken*), premiered on 18 February 1927 in Leipzig at the Neues Theater. It is a light one-act comedy of errors – too light for Weill who, having already collaborated with Brecht on *Mahagonny* in 1927, now returned to work with Brecht on the *Dreigroschenoper* (*The Threepenny Opera*) in 1928. Kaiser's next piece was a romantic love story, *Zwei Krawatten* (*Two Cravats*), 1929, a revue in nine scenes. It received its premiere on 5 September 1929 at the Berliner Theater. Despite its kitschy overtones and the rather conventional music by Mischa Spoliansky, the public loved the show, its lavish production, and the tap-dance numbers by Sammy Lewis. Marlene Dietrich and Hans Albers, one of Germany's most admired light actors, co-starred in the comedy; it was in this production that film director von Sternberg, who was looking for a Lola for *The Blue Angel,* discovered Dietrich.

For his last play staged in Germany before the establishment of the Third Reich, Kaiser collaborated once more with Weill. *Der Silbersee* (*Wintermärchen in drei Akten*) (*The Silverlake, A Winter's Tale in Three Acts*), 1930, is a more topical play which, especially in its songs, satirises Hitler and Nazism. The subtitle *Wintermärchen* is an allusion to Heinrich Heine's cynical cycle of poems about Germany: *Deutschland. Ein Wintermärchen*, 1844. The play was premiered on 18 February in Leipzig at the Altes Theater; the performance was interrupted by a group of stormtroopers who organised a riot similar to that made during the premiere of Toller's *Hinkemann* in 1924. Kaiser had been closely watched by the Nazis since the productions of *Die Lederköpfe* (*The Leatherheads*) which took place on 24 November 1928 at the Neues Theater in Frankfurt, and of *Mississippi* premiered on 20 September 1930 at the Prinzregenten Theater in Munich. The first play openly displays Kaiser's pacifist and anti-fascist attitude; the second dramatises the exploitation of the poor by a ruthless capitalism and pleads for a juster socialism achieved by peaceful means. *Mississippi* played simultaneously in eight more German cities, one of which was Oldenburg where a group of Nazis also tried to bring the play to a halt. Kaiser's impact on the public, like Toller's, could not go unchallenged by the Nazis. As of February 1933 *Der Silbersee* was removed from the repertoire and the staging and printing of Kaiser's works were forbidden in Germany. On 7 May 1933 he was dismissed from the Arts Academy; on 10 May of the same year his books were burned, and on 8 June 1935 he was stripped of his German citizenship. He was denounced as a Jew (which he was not) and as a *Kulturbolschewist* (a cultural Bolshevik). Goebbels himself gave the orders to 'starve Kaiser out' while forbidding the circulation of his works in Germany in any form. Goebbels tried to get Kaiser to write for the Nazi regime, but Kaiser refused his repeated offers; instead he established contact with several underground anti-fascist groups of workers in Berlin. The result was a collection of poems, *Die Gasgesellschaft* (*The Gas Company*), 1936, denouncing Hitler and his ministers in coarse, pornographic language. Photographed copies were circulated through the underground.

Kaiser remained in Germany until 1938 when his stay became too risky. Between 1933 and 1938 he wrote seven more plays, two of which were performed in Vienna in his lifetime. The actor/director Richard Révy invited him several times to move to Switzerland but Kaiser could not finance the trip. In 1935 one of his plays, *Der mutige Seefahrer* (*The Courageous Sailor*) written in 1910, was made into a film, but his authorship was hidden. In 1937 he developed a friendship with the Swiss Expressionist playwright Caesar von Arx, whose works were also forbidden in Germany. Kaiser met von Arx in Berlin in 1938 and after this meeting decided to emigrate to Switzerland.

His remaining years in Swiss exile were a series of restless moves from place to place. After the outbreak of the war, he tried to immigrate to the United States but the American consul in Switzerland refused him entry on the grounds that his sons were serving in the German Army. Besides Caesar von Arx, the writer Julius Marx became Kaiser's closest friend in these years. Marx wrote down his conversations with Kaiser, and they reveal how lonely and desperate Kaiser felt although, again, he quite often distorted reality. He complained repeatedly to his wife about his utter loneliness; on 22 November 1939 he writes to her that it would be better for them not to visit since he could not bear another separation from her. He remarks scornfully: 'You never were – and never will be – exposed to my plights'.[7] This despite the fact that he was living with Maria von Mühlfeld and their daughter. But it is true that his depressions grew together with his misanthropy and his disgust at the Nazi regime. When Germany invaded Holland in 1940, the complete edition of Kaiser's play *Der Schuss in die Öffentlichkeit* (*The Shot at the Public*), 1938, prepared by the emigrant press *Querido* of Amsterdam, was pulped. His play *Der Soldat Tanaka*, 1939–40, which depicts the revolt against war by a simple Japanese soldier and which was premiered by the Zürich Schlauspielhaus on 2 November 1940, was banned.

From 1940 on his health began to fail and his depressions grew to a point where he seriously considered suicide. He sublimates his death wish in *Das Floss der Medusa* (*The Raft of the Medusa*), 1940–3, which surprisingly picks up his Expressionist style. It develops once more the theme of the crucifixion of the New Man. The conclusion is even more cynical than that of his *Gas* plays since the protagonists of the play are children who are shown to be as essentially corrupt as their elders. Kaiser identified himself strongly with Allan, the young protagonist who chooses death rather than survival in a meaningless and corrupt world. His last three plays are the so-called 'Greek' plays: *Zweimal Amphitryon* (*Twice Amphitryon*), 1943, *Pygmalion*, 1943–4, and *Bellerophon*, 1944. In them Kaiser returns to the classical structure of Greek drama and to the timelessness of Greek myth.

Kaiser died on 4 June 1945. Until the very end he was at work on a new novel, *Ard* (only the first chapter is complete), based on what he had learned of the extermination of children in the Theresienstadt concentration camp; he saw a connection between this slaughter and the slaughter of the Innocents by King Herod. Ard, the protagonist, becomes a murderer when his only child is slaughtered by King Herod; his wife commits suicide. Kaiser suggests that Jesus is the one ultimately responsible for the slaughter of the Innocents. This is the real tragedy and meaning of the Christ figure (as Kaiser had already hinted in *Das Floss der Medusa*) – even a pure humanity such as Christ's entails guilt; the New Man he represents is somehow flawed when he engages with a world in which existence is *per se* tragic. One might say that Kaiser had forged his way from the abstractionism of Expressionism to the tragedy of Existentialism.

6

The New Man: Apotheosis and Decline

'Von morgens bis mitternachts' ('From Morning to Midnight')

In 1926 when Kaiser was asked by the newspaper *Svenska Dagbladet* about the genesis of his plays he answered that he felt compelled to 'write about people whom fate had treated unfairly', and that there was hardly a day when he did not encounter a situation which inspired him to write a new play:

> One of my most successful plays *Von morgens bis mitternachts*, for example, was conceived in a strange way. I wanted to travel to Italy and went to my bank for a letter of credit. An old, obviously very poor cashier took care of it. While I was sitting there waiting, I thought that the man was very foolish. Why didn't he steal the letter of credit already made out and travel south himself? Had I a greater claim to enjoy life than

he? Once in Rome, I felt impelled to write a play about
this. (K. 4/592)

Von morgens bis mitternachts is among the earliest
examples of Expressionist *Stationendrama*. It consists of
two parts containing seven stations. The plot is simple and
episodic; in characteristic Expressionist fashion the various
stations which depict a day in the life of the Cashier are only
loosely linked and the action of each station takes place in
different localities. Patterson states that the scenes 'do not
develop from each other in a traditional manner; rather
they give the effect of a montage'. Their order is not
determined 'by the narrative but by the Cashier's development'.[1] The characters are more properly types and have
generic names only – the Cashier, the Lady, the Salvation
Army Girl.

In the first two stations the Cashier, excited by the sight
of a Lady attired in silk and furs and wearing expensive
jewels, steals 60,000 marks from his bank. Convinced that
the Lady is in reality a criminal of some kind and a woman
of easy virtue, the Cashier follows her to her hotel and
offers her the opportunity to escape with him to Italy to a
new and more exciting existence. To his horror he discovers
that she is, in fact, a wealthy and honest woman who rejects
his advances. He flees to a snowfield (third station) where
in a powerful monologue he seeks a meaning to his life.
This scene, the climax and end of the play's first part, is the
best in the play. Its telegraphic style and ecstatic manner
convey well the Cashier's state of fear and excitement
about his future:

> I am really curious. A tremendous feeling of tenseness is
> building up in me. I have reason to think I'm on the brink
> of momentous discoveries. Experiences gained in flight

107

will be invaluable. .... I am prepared to welcome each and every eventuality with open arms. I possess infallible signs that there's an answer for all demands made upon me.   (F.P. 37–8)

He erroneously believes that money can buy him the values he seeks and, in view of the play's end, his words have a double meaning: 'I must pay! – I have the money in cash!! – Where are the goods worth total investments?! Sixty thousand – and the buyer to boot, body and soul? – [*Screaming.*] You must deliver the goods – you must give a fair deal – value for value!!!!' (F.P. 38–9) His question is met (and answered) by a furious storm: '(*His hat is whipped off. The hurricane has lashed the snow from the branches. Remnants stick in the crown and form a human face with grinning jaws. A skeleton hand holds the hat.*)' (F.P. 39). The ensuing 'dialogue' with Death reveals that the Cashier is calculating and cynical; he is a typical Kaiser protagonist, quite unlike Toller's whose motives for action derive mainly from their emotional reactions to situations and fellow humans. Kaiser's heroes are gamblers who, if life does not come up to their expectations, escape into death. At this point, however, the Cashier rejects Death:

I still have various things to settle. When one is on the march, one can't call on everyone. No matter how pressing the invitation. I can see I have a whole lot of calls to make before nightfall. You can't possibly be the first. More likely the last. And even then, only as a last resort – it would hardly be a pleasure. But as I say – as a last resort – well, that's worth considering. Ring me again about midnight.   (F.P. 39)

The four stations of the second part of *Von morgens bis*

mitternachts serve several purposes: they record the Cashier's attempt to buy something of lasting value and they depict graphically the kind of hectic amusement and lack of values Kaiser associates with Berlin. Technically these scenes demonstrate his command of his new style. While each has its own dramatic climax, there exists no essential dramatic link between them. The Cashier's return home is not at all necessary for the development of the play (indeed, it is quite unexpected), but Kaiser takes the opportunity to present a powerful satire on the life-style of the petit-bourgeoisie. The Cashier's two daughters, his wife and his mother live in a stifling environment where their lives revolve around that of the Cashier in his roles as father, husband and son. When he arrives unexpectedly early, he so disrupts their mindless daily routine that the mother dies of a stroke; his departure leaves the rest of his family in a state of shock and indecision.

The Cashier's next station in the sports palace in Berlin probably derives from Kaiser's own love of cycling. Because the Cashier is not at all interested in the sport (he does not even understand the basic rules) this leads to some humorous exchanges quite uncommon in Expressionist drama:

GENTLEMAN: You are a lover of our sport?
CASHIER: I have not the slightest idea what it's all about. What are these fellows down there doing? I see an arena and the line of colour snaking around it. Every so often one comes in and another falls out. Why?
GENTLEMAN: The riders race in pairs. While one is in –
CASHIER: The other chap is out having a good sleep?
GENTLEMAN: Being massaged.
CASHIER: And you call it a six-day cycle race?
GENTLEMAN: What do you mean?

CASHIER: You might just as well call it a six-day cycle
    rest.   (F.P. 48)

The more he watches the excited crowd the more idiotic the
whole thing seems to him. He decides to manipulate the
crowd by offering large prizes but is disillusioned and
disgusted when the mob deserts him and turns into
submissive, silent subjects as the Emperor enters:

CASHIER: The flame that was raging just a moment ago
    has been stamped out by His Highness's patent leather
    boot. You must be mad, to think I am crazy enough to
    throw sixpence to these dogs. Even that would be too
    much. A boot where the dog takes its tail between its
    legs, that's the prize offered!   (F.P. 54)

It was probably because of this 'offensive' speech about the
Emperor that the Prussian censor did not allow the play's
premiere in Berlin in 1917; only after 1918 when censor-
ship was removed after the Emperor had abdicated could it
be staged in Berlin.

    The next station in the Cashier's education, taking place
in a *chambre séparée* of a night club, is grotesquely
humorous. The exchange between the Waiter and the
Cashier ordering dinner is verbal slapstick:

WAITER: Which brand of champagne, sir?
CASHIER (*clears throat.*): Er, Grand Marnier.
WAITER: That is a liqueur for after the champagne.
CASHIER: Oh, then I shall let myself be guided by you.
WAITER: Two bottles of Pommery. Dry?
CASHIER: Of course I am dry.
WAITER: Extra dry?
CASHIER: None of your business but I am; better make it
    three bottles. O.K.

WAITER (*with the menu*): And for dinner?
CASHIER: Pinnacles! (F.P. 55)

The Cashier's attempts to experience an erotic adventure fail. None of the girls ('Female Masks') are what they seem to be; their masks which cover their ugliness are symbolic of the discrepancy between reality and appearance. The Mask whom he invites to dance is the most grotesque – she has a wooden leg.

Although the cycle race and night club scenes seem unrelated and although no explanation is given as to why the Cashier chooses these places, Kaiser introduces a link in the figure of a Salvation Army Girl who appears at regular intervals selling the *War Cry*. It is she who, in the final station, leads him to the Salvation Army Hall. Here, he witnesses the testimonies of several penitents which, in reverse order, retrace the various stages in the Cashier's life. Through these confessions and his growing love for the Salvation Army Girl the Cashier finally discovers the truth about himself: that his search through the various stations of the day have been based on one error of judgment after another: 'I am not hiding anymore, I confess. Not all the money from all the banks in the world can buy anything of real value. You always get less than you pay for' (F.P. 71). But his hope of beginning a new life with the Salvation Army Girl is crushed when he realises that she has betrayed him to the police in order to receive the reward offered for his arrest.

It is typical of Kaiser's irony that the Lady who causes the Cashier to commit a criminal act is in reality an honest character while the Salvation Army Girl who preaches unselfish love and forgiveness is nothing more than a hypocrite. Instead of revelation and transformation the Cashier finds betrayal; furthermore, his discovery that 'of all frauds money is the most miserable' turns out to be ironically true in the fierce battle which emerges for the money which he throws to the 'saved souls' in the Salvation Army Hall. In the final scene the skeleton from the snowfield returns, formed this time by the wires of the chandelier; the Cashier addresses him:

> CASHIER: At the start he is sitting there – stark naked! At the end he is sitting there – stark naked! From morning to midnight I chase round in a frenzied circle – his beckoning finger shows the way out – where to? (*He shoots the answer into his shirt front*.)   (F.P. 73)

Dying he falls with outstretched arms against the Cross sewn on to the curtain of the Salvation Army Hall. The stage directions reinforce the Christ-like association Kaiser intends: '*His dying cough sounds like an "Ecce" – his expiring breath like a whispered – "Homo"* ' (F.P. 73).

Von morgens bis mitternachts sets the tone of most of Kaiser's Expressionist dramas, whose major theme is man's disillusionment and loss of values. Indeed, there are only two of Kaiser's plays which dramatise the triumph of the New Man, namely *Die Bürger von Calais* and *Hölle, Weg, Erde*. The others display in various settings the unwillingness or inability of mankind to become regenerate no matter how persuasive the examples offered to them by the regenerate. Like Toller, Kaiser is again and again attracted to the theme of man achieving a higher self and, like Toller, he is again and again disillusioned by reality. Both authors arrive at the same solution to this disillusionment – escape by the protagonist into death.

Von morgens bis mitternachts was premiered on 28 April 1917 at the Munich Kammerspiele. Otto Falckenberg directed it with Leo Pasetti as designer and Erwin Kalser in the role of the Cashier. Interestingly, Falckenberg did not follow the original division of the play with Part One ending after the snowfield scene, but had the intermission after scene four instead; this may be a more logical division indicating the Cashier's break with his life in a small town and his departure for Berlin. One of the most interesting and most difficult scenes to stage is the snow scene in which the Cashier meets Death. The difficulty arises from the stage directions calling for a gradual metamorphosis to take place in which the tree assumes the appearance of a figure representing Death. Of the many designs César Klein's for the 1921 Barnowsky production in Berlin is by far the most ingenious and by now the best known. Instead of following the stage directions which also called for the Cashier to sit in the tree, he painted a backdrop which fused in Expressionist-primitive fashion images of a tree and a skeleton, towering over the scene and the Cashier alike.

Brecht, who had seen the Falckenberg production in Munich, recognised at once the play's potential as a film, mainly because of Kaiser's numerous 'silent' stage directions which form an integral part of the text. In 1920 the play was made into a film directed by Karlheinz Martin in collaboration with Robert Neppach. Ernst Deutsch acted as the Cashier and Martin's wife Roma Bahn played most of the female roles. It bore many resemblances in staging, sets and lighting to Toller's *Die Wandlung* which Martin and Neppach had staged the previous year. Martin did not use captions; he relied solely on action, design and lighting (black and white). He developed certain photographic techniques including the dissolve. This was especially effective in conveying the omnipresence of death. Martin could not use the snow scene because it depends primarily on speech; however, he did suggest death by having the faces of the women the Cashier meets dissolve into skulls.

Curiously, the film was not accepted by a German distributor and apparently was never released in Germany or elsewhere; it was thought lost until a copy of it was tracked down by Lotte H. Eisner in a Japanese film archive. It was shown for the first time during a seminar on Expressionism held in Frankfurt in 1968.

Von morgens bis mitternachts became Kaiser's most famous and most often produced play, making its way quickly on to the international stage and into various anthologies. However, it took some time to establish itself outside Germany. For example, the production in 1920 at the experimental stage of the London Stage Society was a failure, reviewed as a 'regrettable breach of taste'. The French critics disliked the 'furor teutonicus', the 'ecstasy' and the shouting on stage. The 1922 production in New York at the Theatre Guild, however, was hailed. The English theatre critic and dramatist, Ashley Duke, who had seen the play in Cologne in 1918 with Toller's *Die Wandlung*, Sorge's *Der Bettler* and von Unruh's *Ein Geschlecht*, preferred *Von morgens bis mitternachts*, translating and publishing it in 1920 for an issue of the American literary journal *Poet-Lore. Von morgens bis mitternachts* thus became the first easily available Expressionist drama on the American continent. Its production was carefully planned and timed by the director–designer team of Frank Reicher and Lee Simonson. The play was presented as a special production for subscribers and the press only. However, its success was so overwhelming that the Theatre Guild proceeded to rent the Frazee Theatre on Broadway where it played successfully from June to August 1922. Its success was the more astonishing since the Frazee was normally used to present vaudeville; critics found the play a welcome challenge after the usual light Broadway entertainment. After this production, German Expressionist drama had a foothold in the States and *Von morgens bis mitternachts* was considered to be its best and most representative example.

Kaiser later considered *Von morgens bis mitternachts* as part of a trilogy that included *Kanzlist Krehler* (*Clerk Krehler*), 1921, and *Nebeneinander* (*Side by Side*), 1923. In 1924 he wrote to Hans Theodor Joel:

> *Nebeneinander* is the final play of a trilogy which is not linked by a similar plot or similar figures, but the same summons is sounded three times. . . . Three times, the protagonist is met by a special event – through a simple accident, they are pushed out of their daily routine marvelling into possibilities of boundless extent.
>
> (K. 4/583)

While *Kanzlist Krehler* was only moderately successful, *Nebeneinander* proved a tremendously popular play after its premiere in Berlin in 1923 with sets designed by George Grosz, who was famous for his satirical sketches of the materialistic bourgeoisie of the Twenties.

In *Nebeneinander*, which represents a transition from the Expressionist mode to Kaiser's more realistic (and popular) plays, he has ingeniously interwoven three plots. A Pawnbroker finds a letter in a suit left with him by Neumann in which he begs a certain girl, Luise, not to commit suicide because of her unhappy love for him. When he attempts to return the letter to Neumann, the Pawnbroker is arrested because he wears a pawned fur coat which turns out to be stolen. Since his licence, and thus his livelihood, have been taken away from him, he poisons himself and his daughter. In the other two plots, Luise falls in love with someone else and gets married, while Neumann becomes a successful manager in the film business; he had made it to the top because of his vigour and ruthlessness: 'He has elbows – this Neumann. How his chest nearly splits his tail-coat – phenomenal. He is the type who makes it. When we'll all croak on our last leg, he will still happily whistle "die Wacht am Rhein" ' (K. 2/342). *Nebeneinander* became popular *not* because of the Expressionist elements in the plot which concerns the Pawnbroker's fate, but because of the other two more realistic, and certainly more entertaining, stories. Kaiser sensed this and from then on produced a number of entertaining comedies which seems to contradict his argument in 1922 that true art can only be realised through Expressionism: 'Expressionism means the duration of art. The Platform for Expressionism has been created with an unprecedented vitality. . . . Every reaction is a confession of total defeat. We are experiencing the greatest epoch in art: – Expressionism' (K. 4/572). In 1912 when he wrote *Von morgens bis mitternachts* Kaiser was certainly not aware of his central role in establishing Expressionist art in drama; neither could he know then that his next play, *Die Bürger von Calais*, begun in the same year, would have as protagonist a figure who would always be associated with Expressionist drama – the New Man.

'Die Bürger von Calais' ('The Burghers of Calais')

Kaiser was attracted to the theme of *Die Bürger von Calais* by Auguste Rodin's sculpture *Les Bourgeois de Calais* which commemorates the siege of Calais (1346–7) by the English King, and the heroism of six noble burghers of Calais on their way to surrender the key of the city, and their lives, to Edward III. For the historical background of the events of the siege Rodin had used the account by French historian Jean Froissart as given in his *Chroniques de France, d'Angleterre, d'Ecosse, d'Espagne, de Bretagne*.

Froissart records how the city's inhabitants were saved from being massacred by the wisdom and bravery of their governor, Jean de Vienne, and Eustache de Saint-Pierre, the richest citizen of Calais and leader of the six hostages who were ultimately spared from death through the intervention of the English Queen Philippa. Kaiser also used Froissart's history in writing his play, but in addition it is likely that he was familiar with Rilke's detailed description and interpretation of Rodin's sculpture. (Kaiser admired Rilke who at one time had been Rodin's secretary.) *Die Bürger von Calais* is an interesting example of how the author uses history. While the play in general derives its plot from Froissart's account, the historical background (as in others of Kaiser's 'historical' plays) becomes merely a backdrop against which he dramatises contemporary problems and personal concepts.

The drama opens with the English Officer's message to the burghers of Calais that the King of England is prepared to accept the surrender of the city if 'at dawn six of the Councillors . . . set out from the city – bareheaded and barefoot – clothed in penitent's garb with a rope about their necks' (F.P. 84) and offer themselves as a sacrifice to save the city and its harbour from destruction. In the ensuing debate between Duguesclins, Officer of the King of France (and spokesman for fanaticism and abstract notions of militarism and honour), and Eustache de Saint-Pierre (spokesman for pacifism and moral courage), the latter emerges the winner. He is the first to offer himself as a hostage and is soon joined by other Councillors. Kaiser departs from history in adding a seventh volunteer. Since only six of the seven volunteers must die, Act Two is concerned with determining which one will be spared. Eustache de Saint-Pierre decides to cast lots, coloured balls in a covered dish; however, he has arranged it so that all

117

seven pull the same colour. Kaiser is concerned in this act
with probing the degree to which the volunteers (excluding
Eustache) have committed themselves to martyrdom. How
authentic is their sacrifice? Have they committed themselves to death on the spur of the moment, out of
excitement instilled in them by Eustache de Saint-Pierre's
persuasiveness?

> EUSTACHE DE SAINT-PIERRE: ... Today you seek the
> decision – today you deaden your resolve – today you
> let fever overwhelm your will to act. Thick smoke
> swirls about your heads and feet and shrouds the way
> before you. Are you worthy to tread it? To proceed to
> the final goal? To do this deed which becomes a crime
> – unless its doers are transformed? Are you prepared –
> for this your new deed? It shakes accepted values –
> disperses former glory – dismays age-long courage –
> muffles that which rang clear – blackens that which
> shone brightly – rejects that which was valid! – Are you
> the new men? (F.P. 114–15)

The act ends with Eustache proposing to the other six that
the next morning, at the first stroke of the bell, each one
will set out from his house to the market place, and that the
last one to arrive will go free. This test, unlike a lottery
which depends on chance, will be based on free will and
deliberate moral conviction: in other words, on a true
Wandlung.

The third act brings the climax. One after the other six
hostages and the city's Councillors arrive at the market
place, but not Eustache de Saint-Pierre. The Councillors'
admiration for him turns into rage since they believe that he
has tricked them to save his own neck. As they prepare to
search for him in order to sit in judgment on him, his body is

carried to the market place on a bier shrouded in black. It is followed by his ninety-year-old, blind father who in prophet-like manner explains to the startled crowd why Eustache committed suicide that night:

> He drove on and on to ward off sleep from your eyelids –
> discovered ways and means to draw you closer and closer
> together – sustained you until this morning! . . . He has
> thrown open the last gateway before you. He has cleared
> the darkness of terror and you can pass – with unfaltering
> steps – and unerring feet. Your deed burns about you
> with a clear flame.   (F.P. 128–9)

Eustache's suicide is a final lesson teaching the six hostages how to commit themselves to their deed free from any selfish consideration or human emotion. His death is but the prelude to his resurrection as the New Man:

> THE FATHER OF EUSTACHE DE SAINT-PIERRE: . . . I come out
> of this night – to go into night no more. My eyes are
> open never again to be closed. My blind eyes are sound
> – what I have witnessed I shall never forget: I have
> seen the New Man – This night He was born.
>   (F.P. 130)

While the reversal of the King's verdict which concludes the play is consistent with Froissart's account of how the Councillors were saved, it is also skilfully employed by Kaiser to dramatise his conception of the New Man. The English King spares the city and the volunteers because a son has been born to him that night. If *Von morgens bis mitternachts* ends with symbolism associated only with Christ's crucifixion, the symbolism at the close of *Die Bürger von Calais* quite pointedly suggests both death and

119

resurrection. Eustache's body is carried into the church and placed on the uppermost step:

> *Light floods across the church façade above the door: its lower part represents a deposition from the cross; the frail body of the dead man lies limply in the sheets – six stand bowed over his litter. The upper part depicts the elevation of the dead man: he stands free and untrammelled in the sky – six heads are turned up towards him in wonder.*
>
> (F.P. 132)

Compared to *Von morgens bis mitternachts*, *Die Bürger von Calais* is more typical of Kaiser's Expressionism in both language and content. Although the play consists of three acts and seems to observe the Aristotelian unities, it is, in fact, a *Stationendrama*. Each act can be understood as a separate stage in the development of the theme which is the renewal of man. Each act has its own climax. Act Two, for example, is a little *Stationendrama* in itself in which each of the six Councillors bids farewell to his family and participates in the climactic action of the lottery. Although all the characters of the play are dominated and guided by the protagonist, Eustache de Saint-Pierre, he is not a hero in the Aristotelian sense since he lacks a flaw and his 'antagonists' are patently no match for him. He does not endure any agonising ordeal (he accepts death with stoic equanimity), nor is he influenced by fate; on the contrary, his control of fate is demonstrated by his handling of the scene where all seven men pick the blue balls which signify death (and ultimate resurrection).

Most interpreters compare the character of Eustache de Saint-Pierre to Christ because he sacrifices himself out of love for his fellowmen without expecting anything in return.[2] Although such comparisons are justified, it should be pointed out that Eustache may also be compared with Socrates whose wisdom enlightens his fellow humans and whose death is freely accepted and offered as an example. His death is not only described in Christian imagery, but is also compared to the soul's crossing of the river Styx in Greek mythology:

> THE FATHER OF EUSTACHE DE SAINT-PIERRE: . . . Is it not easy to go where someone calls? The chores are gay with the words of a promise – he calls it out in rejoicing – draws the last of you into the boat. Six oars dip – the keel furrows straight and true: – Your goal steers you more surely than the helm.   (F.P. 128)

The influence of Plato is further seen in the dialectical form of the symposium which shapes *Die Bürger von Calais*. Northrop Frye writes of the symposium's structure that it is 'clearest in Plato, where Socrates is both teacher and lover, and whose vision moves toward an integration of society in a form like that of the symposium itself, to dialectical festivity which . . . is the controlling force that holds society together'.[3] The dialogue of *Die Bürger von Calais*, based on the principle of thesis, antithesis and synthesis, constitutes the action of the play which is otherwise relatively static. The posing of questions in this manner is a particular dynamic device which Kaiser employs in many of his plays. In *Die Bürger von Calais* whole scenes are built on Socratic questions put to the Councillors by Eustache de Saint-Pierre. Indeed, Eustache's role consists in asking questions which are intended to make his friends think and reply.

The most interesting example of how Kaiser develops his dialectical method of argumentation is his almost audacious repetition of a few words which also function as

121

leitmotivs. In *Die Bürger von Calais* the two words *Werk* (work) and *Tat* (deed) are the most significant and the most complex. Kaiser employs these words in a thesis, antithesis and synthesis which is intended to demonstrate how Eustache de Saint-Pierre teaches the Councillors how to turn into new men. At the beginning of the play, in the thesis, *Werk* means the building of the harbour of Calais which the burghers hope to save from destruction through the *Tat* which is represented by the sacrifice of the six Councillors. In the antithesis, however, the protagonist argues that if the *Tat* or deed is contaminated by non-altruistic reasons, the *Werk* or the harbour to be saved will now be hated by the six volunteers who must die to save it. Jean de Vienne, leader of the Councillors, demonstrates this in his speech; the 'deed' must be done but their resolve is overshadowed by their fear of death which is eased only by the hope everyone of the six nourishes that fate will spare him:

> JEAN DE VIENNE: . . . And must it not distress you a hundred times more deeply? – Are you not at the same time free and lost – as long as the choice wavers? As the burden that weighs you down becomes heavier and heavier – do you not have to strengthen your resolve time and again – which from the very first threatens to fade? (F.P. 96)

In the synthesis of Act Three, Eustache's suicide which is an act of total altruism based on moral freedom shows how both the *Werk* and the *Tat* may be reconciled on a spiritual level, and how the New Man can be born:

> EUSTACHE DE SAINT-PIERRE: . . . You court this deed – before it you discard your robes and sandals – it

demands you naked and new-born–around it no battle
clashes – no fire flares – no cry shrieks. You cannot
kindle it with burning ardour or with raging desire. It
burns clear, smokeless flame – cold despite its heat –
gentle in its blinding light. Thus it towers up high – thus
you go your way – thus it accepts you: – unhalting,
unhasting – cool and bright within yourselves – happy
but unfevered – bold but not delirious – willing but not
angry – the new men of the new deed! –   (F.P. 115)

Although *Die Bürger von Calais* belongs among Kaiser's
best and most complex Expressionist plays, it leaves some
questions unanswered. For example, does Eustache de
Saint-Pierre's teaching and suicide really transform the six
Councillors into new human beings? Although they remain
mute during the whole of the third act, their actions (all six
stretch out their hands to carry the key of the city and set
out willingly to meet their death) suggest that they now
accept their fate; nowhere, however, does Kaiser state
clearly that they have changed. Like Toller's, Kaiser's New
Man is an artistic projection of the best in mankind and, as
in the case of Toller, only a few extraordinary human
beings are capable of such a transformation.

In *Die Bürger von Calais* the New Man is clearly depicted
in the character of Eustache de Saint-Pierre. Perhaps he
commits suicide so that the six volunteers can accept their
deaths freely and willingly now that any hope of reprieve
has been taken away by his death. Kaiser's conclusion is
densely ambiguous. This ambiguity is further emphasised
by the contrast between Eustache's moral vision of the New
Man and the historical fact that the war between England
and France continued for another century. One may
question the appropriateness of his suicide (neither Christ
nor Socrates committed suicide). Could suicide in this play

represent a death wish? In *Von morgens bis mitternachts*, for example, the Cashier asks Death: 'Are you an agent of the police? Not in the usual narrow sense. All-embracing! Existential Police? – Are you the definite answer to my probing?' (F.P. 39). At the end of his journey he welcomes death because his 'beckoning finger shows the way out' (F.P. 73). Eustache de Saint-Pierre's death differs from that of the Cashier in that the latter accepts it matter-of-factly, whereas the death of Eustache has ecstatic overtones. Life is compared to darkness while death is associated with light: 'The sevenfold silver brightness shines from every corner – the awesome day of days awaits you! – . . . He prophesied it – and extolled it – and waited joyful and carefree for the bell to ring out the feast – then he raised the cup from the table with steady hands and calmly with steady lips consumed the burning draught' (F.P. 130). While this scene is more reminiscent of the death of Socrates who received the cup cheerfully and drank the hemlock 'readily and calmly' than of the death of Christ who prayed that the cup be taken away from him, it does seem to glorify a death wish (almost a kind of *Todessehnsucht* in the Wagnerian tradition) in a manner that is not present in the accounts of Socrates and Christ.

The most satisfying answer to this question is that after *Von morgens bis mitternachts* Kaiser began to probe death from an existential point of view. This becomes most obvious in *Der gerettete Alkibiades* (1919) (where he explores this aspect further) where, interestingly enough, the play's protagonist is Socrates. One may argue that the figure of Eustache de Saint-Pierre is a forerunner of Kaiser's Socrates, but the latter figure represents a shift from the theme of transformation to an existential theme of life and death. However, despite this new development, Kaiser never lost his fascination with the *Wandlung* theme. As often as he stated how much he despised mankind, as often he repeated how much he believed in man and his possibilities. This somewhat schizophrenic attitude (which is also typical of Toller) is reflected in *Die Bürger von Calais* where the New Man has to die in order to be recognised as such. After this play Kaiser does not employ the term *Der Neue Mensch*; instead he speaks of *Der Mensch* (the man as ideal human) whose characteristics are pacifism, altruism and wisdom.

Die Bürger von Calais was premiered on 29 January 1917 in the Frankfurt Neues Theater, directed by Arthur Hellmer with Eugen Klöpfer as Eustache de Saint-Pierre. With this play began Kaiser's fame as a playwright; three more premieres followed in that same year: *Von morgens bis mitternachts* in Munich, *Die Koralle* in Munich and Frankfurt simultaneously (in Frankfurt once more directed by Hellmer, with Klöpfer in the leading role). Frankfurt Expressionism may be said to date from the 1917 production of *Die Bürger von Calais*. As the Expressionist writer Kasimir Edschmid pointed out, the modern German theatre did not develop in Berlin, but in the provinces. Edschmid also hailed Kaiser as the most promising talent among the new Expressionist playwrights; he was particularly fascinated by Kaiser's use of language, a point made by several other critics. A number of reviewers, however, faulted Kaiser's tendency to abstractionism. One contemporary reviewer, Alfred Polgar, described the atmosphere of the play as 'cold' and 'harsh'; he found the work almost unbearably abstract in form and thought. While he liked the new lighting effects and the stylised choreography of the mass scenes (in the production by John Gottowt, 14 October 1917), he found the play to be a 'torture' because of the complexities of its ideas and language. He argued that the play was a *Lesedrama* (a closet drama) rather than a stage play. There is certainly some truth in this criticism. Because they saw themselves as visionaries heralding the birth of the New Man, Expressionist dramatists often ran the risk of letting ideas overwhelm the action of their plays; *Die Bürger von Calais* strikes a precarious balance between didacticism and art.

'Der gerettete Alkibiades' ('Alkibiades Saved')

> But those who are found to have lived an eminently holy life, these are they, who, being freed and set at large from these regions in the earth, as from a prison, arrive at the pure abode above, and dwell on the upper parts of the earth. And among these, they who have sufficiently purified themselves by philosophy shall live without bodies, throughout all future time . . .   (*Phaedo*.)

Between 1917 and 1919, and again in 1931, Kaiser worked at the play *Der gerettete Alkibiades* which Brecht described as a renewal of the theatre; in his opinion, Kaiser had changed decisively the situation of the European theatre in that he had turned it 'into an intellectual affair'.[4] One may argue that Brecht's criticism was biased since he pursued the same aim in his epic theatre, yet the play has been praised equally highly by others. 'It represents one of the most brilliant works of Expressionism,' writes Sokel, 'illustrating both the Platonic tendency and the basic cultural problems of which Expressionism was one manifestation'. Schürer ranks it, from a stylistic point of view, as Kaiser's 'most Expressionist drama'. Kaiser himself thought highly of *Der gerettete Alkibiades*; on 13 August 1919 he wrote to Otto Liebscher:

I believe – I feel – I know: that I have accomplished the

almost impossible. The whole of Plato in it – the whole of Nietzsche – and everything is integrated into scenes of the liveliest expression. I have recreated Greece – and toppled that of Goethe-Winkelmann. Humanity must thank me – or it doesn't exist.[5]

Yet despite the critics' praise, *Der gerettete Alkibiades* belongs to the lesser known plays of Kaiser's Expressionist period; little is known of its premiere on 29 January in the Munich Residenztheater or of subsequent performances. The fact that Kaiser worked longer than usual at this play may hint at some difficulties in dealing with its philosophical implications. This is reflected in the different interpretations offered by various scholars. Even the play's title is somewhat misleading in that its protagonist is not Alkibiades, but Sokrates.[6] In *Der gerettete Alkibiades* Kaiser explores a topic which concerned him throughout his life: how to combine harmoniously the demands of the intellect with those of the body. Socrates, with whom Kaiser liked to identify, must have seemed to him the ideal character to explore and dramatise this question. The play can be further understood as a tribute to Plato. In a short essay, 'The Drama of Plato, or *Der gerettete Alkibiades*; The Platonic Dialogue', Kaiser argues that the drama of Plato is superior to other forms of drama because 'Discourse spurs objection – each sentence instigates new findings – the Yes elevates itself over its No to a fuller Yes – the climax is of a boundless vitality – and a formed mind swells over the conclusions like God's hands over his creation' (K. 4/544).

The plot of *Der gerettete Alkibiades* derives from Plato's *Banquet* where Alcibiades, one of Socrates' most ardent admirers, is introduced in a short scene. Kaiser also used the description of Socrates' death as found in the *Phaedo*: however, as in *Die Bürger von Calais*, Kaiser rings his own characteristic change on a familiar story. He departs from Plato when, with mordant irony, he shows how Sokrates' achievements are based upon deceit. This confirms once more Kaiser's repute as *Denkspieler*; he himself called the play a *Denk-Spiel*.

Der gerettete Alkibiades consists of three parts, preceded by the lament from Hölderlin's *Hyperion* on the destruction of Athens. The play opens with a conversation among the beautiful young pupils of a wrestling school about the extraordinary beauty and vitality of Alkibiades, the hero of Athens who had successfully fought off the attacking enemy. During the next battle, however, the enemy comes closer to defeating the Greeks and would have captured Alkibiades had it not been for Sokrates, a simple, huncbacked soldier. While retreating through a cactus-field Alkibiades had it not been for Sokrates, a simple, hunch- The excruciating pain makes it impossible for him to flee. Wielding his sword in blind fury he protects the weaponless Alkibiades, and thus rallies the Greeks who finally win the battle. During the ensuing victory celebration in the civic temple, Sokrates is offered the golden wreath for his apparent valour; since the pain hinders him from mounting the steep staircase to meet the Prize-Awarder, and since he does not dare to reveal his secret which would have exposed Alkibiades to ridicule, he in turn offers the wreath to Alkibiades. Again his act is misinterpreted as an act of magnanimity.

The thorn incident is Kaiser's invention which he uses as a literal and symbolic device to develop his theme. Without the thorn in his sole, Sokrates would have continued his uneventful life as a maker (artisan, not artist) of hermae. Hermae are memorials to the dead or the famous, heads sculpted upon a pillar. Kaiser would also have been aware that in their earliest form hermae were heaps of stones constructed in the shape of a phallus in honour of Hermes. Thus the herma in its association with death and art, on the one hand, and life and sexuality, on the other, further reinforces the duality at the heart of the play. With the thorn in his flesh Sokrates develops into a celebrated philosopher, and one who, perforce, must challenge conventional Greek values. It forces him to reject the military and athletic aspects of Greek life for values that are purely intellectual and spiritual. But his new life is not without pain and deprivation. In order to avoid the curious crowd wanting to greet him in his false role as the 'hero', he feels compelled to give up his house and garden in the outskirts of Athens to live in a barren attic apartment. Only his wife Xantippe learns the real reason for his much acclaimed 'courage'.

XANTIPPE: Are you afraid – of your own heroic deed?

SOKRATES: It doesn't exist. I didn't want to save Alkibiades – and I didn't want to give Alkibiades the golden wreath.

XANTIPPE: You saved Alkibiades –

SOCRATES: I – I with my humpback – the last in line – : must they not place me above Alkibiades, who shimmers white in body and armor? Who am I – I who even gave the wreath to Alkibiades – and set myself above reward and thanks that are due to him? – Who am I? – A badly wounded man who drove a thorn into his foot in the cactus field and could not go along in the retreat! –[7]

Since the lie has gone too far to allow him to return to his former life, Sokrates decides to continue saving Alkibiades from ridicule out of pity for the hero to whom honour and physical beauty mean so much. Alkibiades, in turn, is much attracted by the philosopher's 'wisdom'. For example, Sokrates explains to him that the 'heroic' battle was nothing more than a 'battle of arms and legs' and thus strips it of all glory and significance. The hermae which Sokrates sculpts become the symbol for the work of the mind:

> SOKRATES (*looks at him a long time – then at work*): Do you see what I am doing here? – I am making a herma. That is a monument for a person – as you are one for whom monuments will be erected. Your achievement is the victory of arms and legs – will they depict and set up your victorious arms and legs? They cut them off – shape a smooth pediment, and set your head on it. Only the head. What is there to the arms and legs? They run and strike – but the head carries out what is special. That is why I remained behind on the battle-field – and the effect showed itself right away, because my head had been at work – : I was able to save your life – and with your life your Greece – and in addition procure for you the golden wreath!
>
> (p. 224)

The irony, of course, is that Sokrates in championing the spirit over body is again telling lies:

> SOKRATES (*flinging up his arms*): I – pitied him!! – I had to invent – what should not be invented!! – I had to cover the sky – and wither the earth – !! – It was no crime of mine – : Compassion!! – Compassion!! – Compassion!!
>
> (p. 225)

Under the influence of Sokrates, Alkibiades becomes a teacher in the wrestling school; however, his admiration for his master turns into jealousy and eventual hatred when he realises that Sokrates is increasingly overshadowing him. In his opinion, Sokrates has already become a herma in his lifetime. His attempt to have Sokrates seduced by his mistress, Phryne, fails because the thorn hinders Sokrates from stepping down into the bath with her; thus is invented a new kind of love, 'platonic' love. Phryne is overwhelmed by Sokrates' apparent rejection of her; in a perverse act of self-denial she rejects the vitalistic Alkibiades whose sexuality suddenly seems base and disgusting to her: the act is perverse because her love for the herma Sokrates is once more based on deceit and illusion and because it goes against her very nature.

Outraged that the mind has once again won over the body, Alkibiades knocks down the hermae in front of Phryne's house and flees. Sokrates is arrested instead. The school Elders accuse Alkibiades of corrupting the boys at the wrestling school; instead of exercising their bodies for future military tasks the boys have turned into grey-clad contemplatives. In a marvellously dialectical and ironic speech Sokrates leads the Elders to condemn *him* to death and thus, once again, saves Alkibiades. He declines the offer of his friends and pupils to flee, not out of bravery but because the thorn makes it impossible for him to do so; he welcomes death as a deliverance from his pain. In a final ironic stroke Kaiser has the Health-Giver extract the thorn so that in walking freely Sokrates may hasten the action of the hemlock and bring about the death he desires. Once again Kaiser undercuts the Platonic accounts which paint Sokrates as one who seeks death because life is an illusion; in *Der gerettete Alkibiades* Sokrates seeks death as a relief from life 'as from a long sickness' and 'heavy suffering'. Dying, however, he leaves his wife, a midwife, to deliver new life, and a young boy – Plato – emerges as the leader of the boys of the wrestling school.

In *Der gerettete Alkibiades* Kaiser develops further a number of ideas he had introduced in *Die Bürger von Calais*. The concept of the New Man has become more complex. In *Die Bürger von Calais* the protagonist acts of his own free will, but the development of Sokrates into a leading philosopher is caused by an accident which sets forever the course of his life. While Eustache de Saint-Pierre's transformation can be interpreted as an ultimate self-fulfilment, Sokrates' transformation is accompanied by the constant pain of the sting in his flesh. Kaiser has introduced a new note: that of physical disability as a prior condition for intellectual creativity. There is no doubt that Kaiser's Sokrates bears autobiographical traits in that Kaiser had experienced many years of illness and nervous disorder which often led him to contemplate suicide; to be creative was one way of surviving. If he himself was unable to partake in life, Kaiser wrote, his works would transmit his ideas to mankind. In *Der gerettete Alkibiades* Sokrates scorns one of the guests, a poet who would rather be crowned with the blue ribbon of fame while alive than have his herma crowned with it.

The thorn, the most important symbol in the play, represents not only Sokrates' transformation but also the exclusive demands of the spirit which Kaiser once called an 'incurable wound which must not be hurt further' (K. 4/563). The opposition between mind and body is further reinforced by Kaiser's use of the Platonic dialogue which he already employed in *Die Bürger von Calais* and also by his use of symbolism, especially that related to colours, a device which he later perfected in his *Gas* plays. Alkibiades, the ideal of physical beauty and bodily strength, wears shining white armour, his chair is of gold and ivory. The civic temple, representing the glory of a materialistically oriented and war-like Greece has 'glittering walls, and ceiling mirrors in golden green' and 'red marble steps'. The most extraordinary array of colours is associated with the beautiful Phryne whose life as a courtesan is exclusively devoted to the body and to the sexual:

> *Bath chamber. A frieze of animals on a bright green ground. In the center, an oval lattice made of ivory and coral surrounding the depressed bathtub. Door at left – red wood – . . . Phryne wears her hair like a stiff column – gold dust on it. Fingernails and toenails enameled violet. Around her torso a short embroidered coat – her legs in thin silk trousers.* (p. 242)

Similarly, the pupils of the wrestling school are first seen dressed in 'gay cloaks'. In contrast to this is Sokrates whose sober life, dedicated exclusively to matters of the mind, is symbolised by his grey philosopher's cloak and by the grey walls of his dwelling. Under the influence of his teaching, his pupils (including Alkibiades) adopt a grey habit, although, in the case of Alkibiades, the adoption of grey represents only a superficial change – it merely hides the 'glorious nudity beneath'.

Alkibiades' actions (his attempt to debase Sokrates through Phryne, his smashing of the hermae when she fails, and his subsequent flight) reveal that he will never change. If the life of the spirit is at first tempting to him, it later threatens his very existence. When Phryne rejects him for the misshapen, asexual Sokrates, he has a vision of Greece overcome by the hermae which represent death's victory over life:

> ALKIBIADES (*tumbles backward – covers his eyes with his palms*): Hideous growth-seed of scorpions – rank profusion of hermae in a wilderness – : hermae in

rows – hermae in circles – hermae coming out of circles
– hermae coming out of niches – out of gateways – out
of streets – flooding the squares – crowds of crushing
hermae that grin – that are dead and laugh – laughter
of mouths that pulse disembodied – glaring of eyes that
stare glassily – death brought to life – the blood dies
and freezes into eternal ice which does not die and
does not live – hermae attacking – the foe in the city –
occupies streets – squares – gateways – sleep on: –
Alkibiades will save the sleeping city!!!!

(pp. 248–9)

What Alkibiades says about Sokrates is indeed true and
is confirmed by Sokrates himself. Born deformed, always
the 'last in line', now totally incapacitated because of the
thorn, he cries out: 'I am not alive'. Hand in hand with the
development of his mind comes the recognition that the
dichotomy between body and mind is fatal if it is not
bridged; ironically, however, it is the thorn in his flesh
which hinders him from bridging the gap. Goethe's and
Winckelmann's Hellenism had glorified the Greeks' ability
to combine the physical and the spiritual; in Plato's
dialogues the duality represented by Kaiser's opposition of
Alkibiades and Sokrates is rarely apparent. Kaiser's
Sokrates is a bitterly ironic parody of the classical Socrates
and in showing how the hunchbacked maker of death
memorials invented Platonism and idealism, he owes more
to Nietzsche than to Plato. His attempt in the closing scene
of the play to reconcile the two is weak because it is not
dramatically prepared. The reference to the boy Plato
seems to suggest a possible reconciliation of mind and body,
but it is undercut by the sustained irony of the play and the
manner of Sokrates' death.

The death of Sokrates, like Eustache de Saint-Pierre's

death in *Die Bürger von Calais*, is significant for several reasons. It can be understood as self-sacrifice which reinforces the importance of their message for mankind or it can be considered as a suicide – Sokrates welcomes death – which releases him from the pain of existence and lets him escape from the riddle it poses:

> SOKRATES: Am I performing a play for you? Is it a tragedy, or does laughter play a part in it? The actor up on the stage doesn't know – the curious one in the audience doesn't reveal it – how can the mixture be perfect? – Sorrow has tears – joy sheds them – both flow into *one* blissfulness. Who distinguishes? – Not you – and not I – – – – : the great is hidden in the small – and out of trifles things pile up and tower to sublime summits on which snow and sun are united.
>
> (p. 264)

Sokrates' death reveals the futility of his spiritual endeavour for people other than his pupils, as well as his failure to save Alkibiades. This is Kaiser's final ironic twist. Sokrates indeed never saved Alkibiades, neither on the battle field nor from ridicule; on the contrary, Alkibiades in his confusion, brought about by Sokrates' philosophy, has become the laughing-stock of Athens and must flee the city while, ironically, Sokrates is condemned to death for having saved Alkibiades. Sokrates' compassion for this hero of Greece finally destroys both; in that they are tragic figures. Kaiser implies that neither Alkibiades nor especially Sokrates were able to save Greece from destruction. This is supported by his choice of Hölderlin's lament as a prologue.

Der gerettete Alkibiades is a pessimistic play since the dualism between body and mind turns out to be a fatal one;

furthermore, the mind's creations, be they philosophical or artistic, are called into question by their very creator. In a radio address in 1930, Kaiser spoke about his life and work. One statement is particularly striking and in line with his attitude towards his art:

> It is obvious that right now I can't voice anything decisive about the importance of writing. I am not ready yet for any judgments of that kind ... However, I sometimes revolted against that exceptional accomplishment of the mind which is called the poetic *oeuvre*. It represents without doubt the maximum output of human faculty. But it also leads to the most dreadful annihilation of man. I am going to devise a sentence: Life is a disturbance of death. Who disturbs it most? The creative mind. There-fore its annihilation will be the most agonising.
>
> (K. 4/605)

There is in Kaiser an inherent nihilism with which he never came fully to terms. In his semi-autobiographical novel *Villa Aurea* (1939) he offers what now would be termed an existentialist view of life: 'An indescribably deep fear (*Angst*) fills men. Of the nothingness, which is the only truth. We know it all – and yet never want to know it' (K. 4/742). *Der gerettete Alkibiades* is Expressionist in deal-ing with the transformation motif and in hailing the best in man, what makes him partake of immortality: his creative mind. But in its questioning of creativity's value and thus man's immortality the play also displays existentialist features which transcend Expressionism.

7
Technology and Armageddon

'Die Koralle' ('The Coral')

I have taken sides with mankind. I can't defend God any
longer.   (K. 4/630)

Although *Die Koralle* is generally considered Part One of
the *Gas* trilogy, it is almost certain that when Kaiser wrote
the play during the years 1916 and 1917 he did not intend
to expand it into a trilogy. *Die Koralle* stands as a drama in
its own right, the conflict which it poses is solved, it also
differs considerably from the two *Gas* plays in style.
Furthermore, Kaiser wrote two different plays, *Der Brand
im Opernhaus* (*The Fire in the Opera House*) and *Der
gerettete Alkibiades,* before he turned to *Gas I* in 1917.
However, there are points of comparison which have led
critics to group these plays in what has come to be known as
the *Gas* trilogy: they deal with four generations of the same
family; there are a number of linking symbols such as the
red coral and the red gas; the two *Gas* plays develop in

137

much more detail the social theme briefly treated in *Die Koralle*. The three plays represent a coherent and progressively pessimistic vision of society in Germany in the past, the present and the future.

Despite the traditional structure of *Die Koralle*, which is in five acts, it belongs clearly in the 'ecstatic' phase of Expressionist drama. The characters or *Figuren* do not have proper names; Kaiser instead of personalising his *dramatis personae* defines them by their social function: Millionaire, Secretary, Doctor, Chaplain, and so on. The play is concerned once again with examining the concept of the New Man and the possible moral renewal of society, here German society, at the end of the nineteenth century. Opposed to the capitalistic Millionaire is a variety of figures, chiefly the Son, whose views clash with those of the Millionaire and provide the intellectual debate at the centre of the play. A complementary, perhaps the overriding, theme is the Millionaire's search for happiness; it provides the drama's emotional centre.

Die Koralle opens with the Millionaire's Secretary distributing money to the needy as he does once a month on an 'open Thursday'. The Secretary is the Millionaire's exact double; only the piece of coral which the former wears at his watch-chain tells them apart. Except for the two Footmen and the Gentleman in Grey no one is aware that the Millionaire and the Secretary are two different people. With the help of the Secretary, the Millionaire can fulfil his need to escape from reality and lead a sheltered life. After his father, a poor worker in the same factory the Millionaire now owns, abandoned his family, his mother took her life. The Millionaire's life has been a never ending flight from his past. He uses his wealth as protection against a pathological fear of reality and he attempts to recapture the happy childhood he never had through his children, especially through his Son. For this reason he has brought up his Son and Daughter away from all contact with the 'dark sides' of life. But his world begins to crumble after they reject his way of life. The Son, instead of travelling on his father's luxury yacht, becomes a stoker on a coal steamer in order to experience the conditions of the workers; the Daughter becomes a nurse caring for the sick workmen of her father's factory. When he sees his hope of redeeming his own past through his children shattered, the Millionaire breaks down:

> I'll pay with my wealth – I'll give away my life for another life!! (*Fervently*.) Who will lend me his, that is bright from the first day on?! – I shall no longer find it in my son – down there! – Now where does the exchange beckon that I longed for in the fever of work – in the frenzy of gain – on the mountain of my illimitable gold?! – In whom can I submerge – and lose this fear and raging turmoil? – Who has a life – serene and smooth – for mine?!! (F.P. 168)

After the Secretary tells him about his own happy child-hood, the Millionaire shoots him; he takes the coral as if, somehow, it will bring with it the happy childhood he never had. Because of the coral, however, he is mistaken for the Secretary, found guilty and condemned to death for murdering the Millionaire. So desperate is he to recapture the unredeemable past that he rejects the Son's offer of freedom and the Priest's offer of salvation. Like Sokrates in *Der gerettete Alkibiades* he chooses death freely and deliberately:

> The turmoil rages and drags us into the frenzy of life. We are all driven onwards – all driven out of the paradise of

our tranquillity. Pieces torn off the coral-tree down there in the dim light – with a wound from the very first day. It doesn't heal – it smarts – our dreadful pain lashes us on our headlong career. (F.P. 192)

In *Die Koralle* Kaiser balances the theme of the possible moral regeneration of humanity against that of the Millionaire's search for happiness. The degree of Kaiser's irony may be deduced from the fact that the play ends, not with the triumph of the New Man and a vision of Utopian future, but with the triumph of the Millionaire who, viewing existence as meaningless and full of horror, escapes through death. This ending is hinted at in the mocking irony of the opening scene where, when the Secretary gives the Young Lady in Taffeta, a former prostitute, a two-year pass to the state's Homes for Fallen Women, she cries out ecstatically: '– I shall become a new being – a new being – !' (F.P. 136).

The theme of *Wandlung* is most clearly established in the treatment of the Millionaire's Son and Daughter. Both come to reject their father because of his wealth and because of the brutality he practises towards his workers after a mine explosion. The Son's experiences among the stokers on the *Albatros* lead to his transformation:

SON: Like scales it fell from my eyes. All the wrongs we do became obvious to me. The rich like us – and the others choking in smoke and torment – and are human beings the same as we are. We haven't the faintest right to do it – why do we do it? (F.P. 156)

The Daughter, too, experiences a *Wandlung* when she touches the Chinese stoker who had collapsed from the heat of the boiler room; her language describing that experience draws heavily on Christian symbolism:

140

When I took my hands off the burning chest of the
Chinese stoker, they bore the stigma. The stigma has
sunk into my blood and into my very heart. I no longer
have any choice. I sense my destiny. And I accept it
willingly. You shall show me the place where I can fulfil
it.   (F.P. 161)

Lest one take the Son and the Daughter at face value
Kaiser has introduced other characters and ideas which
qualify their position. That the Millionaire is driven to
suicide by his Son's transformation is a further ironic twist
on this theme. Kaiser's treatment of the Gentleman in Grey
is another example of his satire on the transformation
theme. The Gentleman in Grey is a type of the doctrinaire
socialist who in the opening act voices ideas associated with
the New Man; by the end of the play he too experiences a
Wandlung but of a different type. By heeding the advice of
the Millionaire he has become a rich man who will continue
to propagate his ideas:

THE GENTLEMAN IN GREY: I bless you. Out of rosy clouds
   you have brought me down to earth. I am planted
   upright on my two firm feet. Your law holds good: we
   are in flight! Woe betide anybody who stumbles. He is
   trodden under foot – and the stampede goes rushing
   on over him. There is no quarter given and no mercy.
   Onwards – onwards! Behind us chaos!   (F.P. 186)

Kaiser also tests the idea of mankind's regeneration in
the Museum Curator of *Die Koralle*. Like the Millionaire
he advocates a complete break with the past; his museum
will have nothing but empty walls as a 'stimulus to new
achievement' (F.P. 151). He considers the past as a burden
which 'weighs us down like a cross – . . . which we shall only

throw off with violence and crime – if need be!' (F.P. 151).
Kaiser does not totally reject this attitude which reflects the
ideas of the first Futurist Manifesto (1909), but he voices
his reservations through the Doctor:

> DOCTOR: Is that possible – without self-deception?
> MUSEUM CURATOR: I don't know.
> DOCTOR: I fear that bearing this cross is inescapable.
> MUSEUM CURATOR: One must desire the future relent-
>   lessly.
> DOCTOR: That may be possible in your gallery.
> MUSEUM CURATOR: More than that I do not claim.
> DOCTOR: In life, I think, no one will be able to leap over
>   his own shadow.   (F.P. 151)

In this exchange Kaiser dramatises the dilemma of the
Expressionists' vision of the New Man. If the vision is ever
realised it can only be within the confines of the ivory tower
(or the museum gallery, or the Millionaire's oval room with
invisible doors), remote from reality. The New Man errs in
thinking that mankind can be changed for the better; 'man
becomes only what he already is', Toller argued.

The transformation of the Millionaire is the most interesting in the play and the one which receives the most
elaborate treatment; his progress is an attempt 'to leap over
his own shadow'. Life is horror, he declares to the
Gentleman in Grey and he has become a Millionaire in
trying to flee from that horror. He can only find peace in
identifying with an *alter ego*: 'You find a continuation with
yourself in your son – while he is himself a beginning' (F.P.
146). The white oval room, the 'warm heart of the earth'
and the white yacht, *Freedom of the Seas*, symbolise his
search for a happiness that is associated with the innocence
of the boy of eight before he encountered the horror of life.

At the play's opening the Millionaire has achieved peace through identification with his son's sheltered life, but he is aware how precarious it is:

> People are always being born who are more deeply terrified. The cause is no longer important. It has always been the lever which applies itself. Progress – the point is not where to – but: what from! – . . . Where do great men come from who conquer the world? They rise up out of the darkness, because they come from the darkness. They experience horror there – one way or another. They are hideous meteors that flare up – and fall!
>
> (F.P. 144)

When he loses his Son he loses also his identity and must search for a surrogate who can lend him a new life 'that is bright – from the first day on'. The Secretary who 'had the greatest of possessions . . . the vivid memory of a happy youth' becomes the surrogate. In taking the coral from his exact double the Millionaire becomes the Secretary; illusion and reality seem to fuse. The transformation that takes place here is unusual in Expressionist drama, for it does not spring from a spiritual change but derives rather from identification with a physical object, the coral. At first sight the coral is identified with the Secretary whose happy youth is compared to 'a lake, whose clarity reflects the blue sky' (F.P. 169). The Millionaire associates it with a pre-lapsarian Eden, 'the paradise that lies behind us' (F.P. 192). But the coral may also be seen to represent something negative, something regressive. 'The thing looks like a drop of blood that has stuck to the culprit' remarks one of the Examining Magistrates. Its blood-red colour associates it with murder; the sea in which it grows represents annihilation and the rejection of the adult world of experience. In the exchange with the Chaplain the Millionaire refuses the cross because it merely 'deadens the pain' of existence in favour of the coral which 'delivers us from suffering' (F.P. 192). The dreadful pain of existence can only be allayed by death. 'What is the best thing to do?' the Millionaire asks the Chaplain and he reflects, 'Not come to the surface and be drawn into the storm as it sweeps us towards the coast' (F.P. 192). The existential wound that is the coral is like the thorn in the flesh of Sokrates.

In the characterisation of the Millionaire Kaiser clearly develops a view at odds with his early concept of the New Man. His *Wandlung* ends in nihilism while the Son's *Wandlung* later leads him to unhappiness and defeat. Kaiser seems more sympathetic to the Millionaire than to the Son – he is said to have identified himself strongly with the Millionaire – and the truth which he arrives at becomes the preface to *Gas I*:

> MILLIONAIRE: . . . But the most profound truth is not proclaimed by you and the thousands like you – only the single individual ever discovers it. And then it is so overwhelming that it becomes powerless in its effect! –
> (F.P. 191)

'Gas I'

I have glimpsed humanity – I must save it from itself!
Gas I

Kaiser's two plays, *Gas I* and *Gas II*, constitute his major contribution to German Expressionist drama. They are the best example of his own maxim that 'writing drama means: to pursue an idea to the end' (K. 4/579). In them he once

144

again explores the possibility of establishing a new political system, socialism, within a regenerated industrialised society. Toller had examined the same possibility in his first three plays and had concluded that the New Man would be born only in a changed society in the distant future. Kaiser ultimately arrived at a more radical conclusion. Despite the occasional appearance of the New Man in the course of history (Jesus, Socrates), Kaiser came to feel that human nature could not be changed for the better, that it was intrinsically corrupt. Jesus, 'a genius of social humanity', demonstrates what happens to the regenerated man: he is hung on a cross and his teachings are futile because: 'an ethical person does not need religion – for the others it's ineffectual'. 'One cannot change man', Kaiser concludes, 'One can only fear him and outdo him in his destructive work' (K. 4/630).

The *Gas* trilogy develops this pessimistic conclusion with relentless logic. In *Gas I*, the Millionaire's Son of *Die Koralle* has begun his altruistic work full of hope and in the conviction that he can ameliorate the social conditions of the proletariat. The play demonstrates the futility of his efforts to convert the workers from the making of gas and the tyranny of machines to a pastoral way of life. It ends with the Son's disillusionment but also with a prophecy – made by his daughter – of the birth of a man who will protect his legacy. This man, the great-grandson of the Millionaire, becomes the protagonist of *Gas II* and he represents Kaiser's final and most terrifying dramatisation of his pessimism and his nihilism. Rejected by the workers who choose instead the Chief Engineer – symbol of technology – the Millionaire-Worker kills himself and his fellow workers with the ultimate poison-gas weapon and so brings about a universal and apocalyptic destruction. The Christ-like New Man of *Die Bürger von Calais* finally metamorphoses into as brutal a figure as the God of technology and Eustache de Saint-Pierre's private act of suicide becomes the collective suicide of mankind. The *Gas* plays represent the darkest and most misanthropic vision of Expressionist drama.

Gas I opens with the description of the Son's office; it had been his father's but there are a few significant changes. In the place of the old 'brown tinted photographs showing factory buildings' there now hang 'wall charts covered with graphs'. The old photographs were reminders of the Millionaire's wealth; the new graphs are indicators of a modern, socialistic system of production where the workers share in the profit and, ironically, work even harder than in the old factories of capitalism. The irony is further underlined by the fact that the product of the socialistic experiment is gas. In the opening scene The White Gentleman (a figure of death) raises the possibility that the gas may be dangerous:

THE WHITE GENTLEMAN: And supposing the gas should – explode?

(CLERK: *stares at him.*)

THE WHITE GENTLEMAN: What happens then?

(CLERK: *speechless.*)

THE WHITE GENTLEMAN (*whispering right in his face.*): The white terror! (*Straightening up – listening to the sounds from overhead.*) Music. (*Stopping half-way to the door.*) Waltz. (*Goes off, noiselessly.*) (F.P. 197)

As Kaiser skilfully juxtaposes home and factory (the Son's daughter is being married to the Officer), the gas begins to turn red in colour. The Engineer's assertion that the formula for the gas is flawless, that his calculations are correct, suggests that the technological process is now

beyond human control, it has turned into a devouring
Moloch:

> ENGINEER: Right – and not right! We have reached the
> limit. Right – and not right! No mathematics will
> penetrate beyond it. Right – and not right! The
> calculation continues on its own reckoning and
> rebounds on us! Right – and not right.   (F.P. 201)

The explosion which, according to science, cannot happen
takes place and the factory is destroyed. In *Die Koralle* the
explosion which occurs is merely reported in the opening of
Act Three; in *Gas I* it takes place on stage: '(*A hissing
sound shatters the stillness outside – briefly a rending
thunder crashes out: the chimney-stacks split and topple.
Smokeless silence. The great window rattles into the room
with a hail of splintered glass*.)' (F.P. 201). The stage effects
are dramatised in the horrifying vision of the dying
Worker:

> Report from shed eight – control room: white cat jumped
> – red eyes staring – yellow mouth gaping – crackling back
> arched – grows round – snaps girders – lifts the roof off –
> and bursts in sparks!! . . . Drive the cat away – shoo,
> shoo!! – hit it on the mouth – shoo, shoo!! – cover its
> scorching eyes – flatten its arched back – every fist on its
> back – look, it's puffing itself out – it's getting fatter and
> fatter – with gas from every pipe and cranny – !! . . . .
> Report from control-room: – the white cat is exploding!!
> (F.P. 202)

The Millionaire's Son, realising that his new social
experiment has not liberated the workers as he had hoped,
proposes that they abandon the gas-production and settle

on farms. There they would live in a more human fashion removed from the slavery of the production line. Kaiser ranges through the gamut of his characters or figures, testing their values against the Son's idealism. The Clerk refuses to accept any other way of life; the Engineer, seduced completely by technology, prefers to resign when asked to stop producing gas; the Officer who has gambled away his wife's dowry shoots himself in accordance with a bourgeois code of honour rather than accept the Son's offer to work on the settlement. The conflict between the Son's humanitarian concern and the cynicism of the prevailing technological society is caught graphically in the confrontation between the Son and the five Gentlemen in Black who represent world capitalism:

MILLIONAIRE'S SON (*staring*.): – Have you forgotten – Have you grown deaf – is the crash no longer thundering in your ears – are you no longer swaying on your chairs – have you lost your faculties??

SECOND GENTLEMAN IN BLACK: The disaster is a dark episode –

FOURTH GENTLEMAN IN BLACK: We book it –

FIFTH GENTLEMAN IN BLACK: – and turn the page!

MILLIONAIRE'S SON: – The same formula – ??

FIRST GENTLEMAN IN BLACK: We hope –

SECOND GENTLEMAN IN BLACK: Of course!

MILLIONAIRE'S SON: – The same formula – ??

THIRD GENTLEMAN IN BLACK: Perhaps there will be longer periods between –

FOURTH GENTLEMAN IN BLACK: We must learn by experience!

MILLIONAIRE'S SON: Twice – three times – ??

FIFTH GENTLEMAN IN BLACK: Then we shall know the cycle!

SECOND GENTLEMAN IN BLACK: At any rate we shan't live
    to see it! (F.P. 219)

The Son's final appeal is to the workers in the climactic
fourth act where he and the Engineer battle for their souls
in the great domed hall lit by industrial arc-lamps. Kaiser's
handling of the crowd scene is a good example of Expressionist abstractionism; the masses are represented by
single figures such as the Girl, the Mother, the Woman, the
Worker, who, though nameless, achieve a haunting individuality because of their vulnerability. Each recites the
story of his plight; each story is individual yet representative, and each tale provides further ironic qualification of
the Son's belief that his socialism can alleviate human
misery. The profit-sharing he had introduced has changed
the workers into robots; they have become dehumanised
by their function. The Girl's brother (now dead) had been
reduced to one hand 'that raised and lowered the lever –
minute by minute up and down – reckoned to the second!'
(F.P. 223). The Mother's son had become 'two eyes, glazed
with the staring at the gauge', and the Woman's husband,
after only one happy day in their life, their wedding day, is
again tied to the trolley: 'The man moves with it – because
the foot is attached to him. Only his foot matters – pushing
the gear-pedal – for stop and start – then pushing and
pushing without the man who moves with it' (F.P. 225).
The Worker cries out, 'Mother – I sacrificed myself for a
gauge no bigger than a finger' (F.P. 226).

At the height of this vast choric cry for justice the Son
and the Engineer make their appeal to the workers – the
one to humanistic ideals, the other to ingrained habit and
self-interest. The workers ultimately prefer gas to the blade
of grass offered them by the Son. They return to the
production line because they lack the vision and imagina-

tion to seize their freedom; the government takes over the rebuilding of the plant and the production of gas. The play ends with the Son's anguished questions addressed to his daughter:

> ... Tell me: ... where is humanity? When will man make his appearance – and call himself by name: – man? When will he comprehend himself – and shake his perception down from the branches? When will he conquer the curse – and re-new creation that he corrupted: – humanity? (F.P. 241)

The Daughter's answer, 'I will give him birth!' which is the closing line of the play, acts as a bridge into *Gas II* as if to suggest that the renewed man will eventually emerge triumphant in the final play of the trilogy.

Diebold's description of Kaiser as a *Denkspieler*, with its connotation of the playwright as a thinker who deals only in the theoretical, neglects the fact that Kaiser, if not as overtly political as Toller or Brecht, was profoundly afflicted by the problems of his time. *Gas I* derives its provenance from the assembly-line method of industrialisation introduced by Ford into his factories, the profit-sharing experiment of the Zeiss factories in Jena, the strike of the ammunition workers in Kiel and Munich in 1918.[1] Furthermore, Kaiser's vision of a more humane life for the factory workers in a pastoral setting is obviously based on G. Landauer's model of a workers' co-operative with which Kaiser was well acquainted. *Gas I* also reflects his apprehension about the imminent Revolution. One day before its outbreak, on 7 November 1918, he wrote to Landauer: 'What will happen? Will it be dawn? – or Explosion? Will there be millions of individuals? – or only millions??'[2] The fifth act of *Gas I* and especially the Son's confrontation with the Gentlemen in Black offer a remarkably clear and intelligent analysis of the way in which capitalist governments manipulated workers and industries. It is ironic that the military should repossess the Millionaire's Son's factory because earlier he had invoked the power of the State to prevent the workers from rebuilding the factory. Toller attacked the government of the Weimar Republic and fought for immediate reforms for the working class of his time, but Kaiser went further. His criticism in *Gas I* is directed against government as such.

Gas I was premiered simultaneously on 28 November 1918 in the Düsseldorf Schauspielhaus, directed by Gustav Lindemann, and in the Frankfurt Neues Theater with director Arthur Hellmer, designer Robert Neppach, and Carl Ebert in the leading role. Hellmer was familiar with Kaiser's works since he had already staged *Die Bürger von Calais* and *Die Koralle*; in 1919 he was to direct *Hölle Weg Erde*, and *Gas II* in 1920. It is clear from contemporary reviews that the roles of the Son and the Engineer were played in an abstract and static fashion, like two poles between which the mass of the workers fluctuated. Both characters were represented as types (which they are in the play), one as the wise 'preacher of ideas', the other as an 'allegory and ghost of materialism'. After a number of problems with the Prussian censor, Kaiser finally managed – with the intervention of Georg Landauer – to have the play performed in Berlin. It opened on 25 February 1919, four days after Kurt Eisner's assassination in Munich, at the Volksbühne, which was then under the directorship of Friedrich Kayssler. It was directed by Paul Legband, with Ernst Stahl-Nachbaur in the role of the Millionaire's Son. Karl Jacob Hirsch designed the set for the play. Kaiser was particularly fond of Hirsch's designs which he once described as *fabelhaft* (marvellous). It was the Volksbühne production of *Gas I* that brought Kaiser the acceptance by the Berlin public he had long sought; despite his statements to the contrary, he was always eager to see his plays performed, and he saw Berlin as the last hurdle. In a letter of 6 June 1918 to Landauer he writes: 'I beg you to make use of *Gas* wherever you want to; its representation on stage is unimportant – its mentioning in your book is infinitely more precious'.[3] A month later he is 'grateful' that Landauer wanted to establish contact with the Volksbühne in order to promote *Gas I*.

Despite generally favourable criticism there were reservations. H. Jhering's review of the Volksbühne production is especially interesting because it is somewhat at variance with the concept of Kaiser as *Denkspieler*. Jhering saw Kaiser as a sensationalist interested primarily in ideas for their colour and variety but not necessarily for their truth. The political issues of his time interested Kaiser certainly, he argues, but again primarily for what use could be made of them in the theatre. Kaiser is doctrinaire in that his plays are based on premises that are postulated as true; his art is mathematical and schematic in its ordering of ideas but the elegance of the complete design is not sufficient to compensate for the lack of drama and the substitution of intellectualised debate growing out of premises that have not been examined or developed. Jhering felt the Daughter's promise that she would give birth to the renewed Man to be gratuitous as there is nothing in the play that prepares one for such a conclusion. Diebold's remark in his review of Hellmer's 1918 production, 'One hoped for Karl Marx but it turned out to be Schopenhauer', also suggests that in *Die Koralle* and *Gas I* Kaiser had not been completely successful in fusing the political and philosophical levels of the plays. *Gas II* does, however, represent a successful fusing of both levels but the nihilism of the play's horrific ending far transcends the class struggle inherent in Marx's historicity and the pessimism of Schopenhauer's philosophy.

'Gas II'

The earth is the creation of a madman. In our most loathsome actions we resemble this creator most.

(K. 4/631)

Gas II was written against the backdrop of the end of the First World War, the defeat of Germany and the signing of the Treaty of Versailles. It was deeply influenced by the contemporary political unrest in Germany, specifically that in Munich, and by the murders of Liebknecht, Luxemburg and especially those of Landauer and Eisner: the latter became the model for the Millionaire-Worker of *Gas II*. Toller's imprisonment added to Kaiser's pessimism about the future of Germany. Much of this is reflected in the vision of doom offered in the last play of the *Gas* trilogy. The world war predicted in *Gas I* now takes place, the production of gas is controlled by a government whose representatives are the Blue Figures; the enemy is represented by sinister Yellow Figures who are attacking when the play opens. While the Yellow Figures are more numerous, the Blue Figures are technologically superior.

In the first act the First Blue Figure asks the Millionaire-Worker (the great-grandson of the Millionaire of *Die Koralle* and the regenerated man promised by the daughter at the close of *Gas I*) to fire up the Workers to greater efforts in producing gas that will ultimately lead to universal destruction. The Millionaire-Worker refuses and the act ends with the Workers going on strike as they cry out, 'Kein Gas!!!!'

Act Two is a sublime statement of the possibilities open

to the Workers when, under the direction of the Millionaire-Worker, they attempt to send a message of peace to the enemy – the Yellow Figures. But as the assembled Workers again cry out, 'Kein Gas!!!!', the Yellow Figures invade the factory and force them to return once again to the manufacturing of gas. In the third and final act the Chief Engineer, who has discovered an ultimate weapon, a poison gas, urges the Workers to use it against the enemy although this may mean mutual destruction. As in *Gas I* Kaiser has the idealist and the technologist clash before the Workers in a struggle for their allegiance:

> MILLIONAIRE-WORKER: Set up the kingdom whose rule is omnipotent in you!
>
> CHIEF ENGINEER: Calculate the power that will be your prize. Works and profits will be yours – without a single finger's lifting. Gas will work for you as if by magic – your serfs will be held fast at the lever – the gear pedal – before the gauge. You will use the victory after the example set by yesterday's victors!
>
> MILLIONAIRE-WORKER: Liberate yourselves in suffering from slavery that touches nothing within you!
>
> (F.P. 270)

The Engineer wins and now the Workers roar in unison, 'Giftgas!!!!' Rejected by his fellow Workers the Millionaire-Worker smashes the sphere which contains the deadly gas and destroys them; so lethal is the gas that it drives the Yellow Figures mad and into a collective suicide. The final scene of the play is as effective and disturbing as any in Expressionist drama:

> YELLOW FIGURE (*checks – crazed glance wanders – shouts into the telephone.*): Reporting effect of bombard-

154

ment: turn the guns against yourselves and annihilate
yourselves – the dead are thronging from their graves –
judgement day – dies irae – solvet – in favil – (*He
shoots the rest in his mouth*.) (*In the haze-grey distance
clusters of fireballs hurtle against each other – clearly in
self-destruction*.)   (F.P. 272)

Gas II is perhaps the most abstract drama in the
Expressionist canon. Diebold's reaction to the Hellmer
production on 23 December 1920 in the Frankfurt Neues
Theater reflects the shock caused by the play upon public
and critic alike: '*Gas*, part two, is the leanest drama in
world literature: a skeleton. . . the tendency to *Telegrammstil* and to the total de-individualising of all that is human
has led to the withering away of drama. Its structure: the
skeleton of a machine; the characters: its functioning
parts.'[4] The language of the play also mirrors its skeletal
functionality. Kaiser strips it of adjectives, articles and
conjunctions where possible; the fast succession of nouns
creates tension and the use of short, staccato an-
nouncements in the opening scene of the first act quickly
establishes an appropriate sense of foreboding and fear.
The stark setting, reminiscent of cubist art, reinforces
dramatic structure and language: a cluster of red and green
wires which descend from the dome of a concrete hall are
distributed to small iron tables; the cold mechanical effect
they create is heightened by the green and red lights from
panels which illuminate the faces of the Blue and Yellow
Figures at their computer-like operations. Except for a part
of the second act, the stage is lit by harsh arc-lamps.

In *Gas II* Kaiser has further dehumanised his figures; no
longer are they defined by their social function but only by
colour as if to indicate the degree to which a ruling class can
become ruthless and interchangeable. His use of colours

155

may owe something to Kandinsky's theory of the inter-relationship of sound, movement, colour and mental associations developed in his *Über das Geistige in der Kunst* which he applied in his play, *Der gelbe Klang* (*The Yellow Sound*).[5] Kandinsky's theory was well known in Expressionist circles: the painter Franz Marc, for example, explained that he had used the colour yellow for his famous picture, 'Der Tiger', because this colour best expressed the animal's aggressiveness. Similarly, Kaiser's Yellow Figures are the aggressors while the Blue Figures suggest dehumanisation and clinical detachment. It is also possible that Kaiser associated his Blue and Yellow Figures with phosgene gas (blue) and mustard gas (yellow) which were 'planned to be used' towards the end of the First World War.

The three acts of *Gas II* are constructed in symmetrical fashion. The Blue Figures of Act One are replaced by the Yellow Figures of Acts Two and Three; the language and actions of both Figures are virtually identical and portray the same mindless devotion to technology. Kaiser emphasises the play's symmetry by a careful patterning involving numbers. There are three workshops producing gas, three battle sectors, three supply depots, and the enemy's attack is in three phases. In Act Two when the message offering peace is sent through the opened dome, the action is carried out in three stages: 'Roll the dome clear', 'Rig the antenna', 'Send out the signal'. In Act One the production of gas falls twelve units below quota as it does in Act Three.

The careful, even mathematical, structuring of Acts One and Three is balanced by the style which provides many prime examples of Expressionist *Telegrammstil* – a style that is here cold and scientific, divorced from any human concern:

SECOND BLUE FIGURE (*before red-glowing panel*): Report from third battle-sector: enemy concentration growing.

(*Panel-light fades.* FIRST BLUE FIGURE *crossplugs red contact.*)

FIFTH BLUE FIGURE (*before green-glowing panel*): Report from third workshop: production one point below quota.

(*Panel-light fades.* FIRST BLUE FIGURE *crossplugs green contact.*)

THIRD BLUE FIGURE (*before red-glowing panel*): Report from second-battle sector: enemy concentration growing.

(*Panel-light fades.* FIRST BLUE FIGURE *crossplugs red contact.*)

SIXTH BLUE FIGURE (*before green-glowing panel*): Report from second workshop: production one point below quota.

(*Panel-light fades.* FIRST BLUE FIGURE *crossplugs green contact.*)

FOURTH BLUE FIGURE (*before red-glowing panel*): Report from first battle-sector: enemy concentration growing.

(F.P. 245)

Act Two is in deliberate contrast to Acts One and Three; it is a magnificent celebration of the possibilities open to the Workers – now briefly liberated – and both setting and language suggest freedom and rebirth. The action takes place in the concrete hall but now the industrial harsh arc-lights are diminished and give way to the light of the sun when the dome of the hall is rolled back. The representative figures – Girl, Young Worker, Man, Old Woman – speak wonderingly of their new freedom in a language which, in contrast to the *Telegrammstil* of Acts One and

Three, is highly poetic and ecstatic, charged with imagery drawn from nature:

> YOUNG WORKER (*up on to the platform to the GIRL*):
> Morning for you and for me that fuses into our fulfilment. The living and longing made up of day after day is empty without the existence of you and me until morning, splendid and radiant. – Now the torrent breaks through the flood-gates spilling out over the banks that gain a new meaning! islet abundant with colour and sounds of a wedding! (F.P. 254)

Under the direction of the Millionaire-Worker the dome is rolled back and a broad shaft of light illuminates the hall. The light is a 'lambent pillar' (like the pillar of fire which led Moses out of servitude) and the Workers stand in 'Dazzled silence – all faces upturned' (F.P. 259). The moment of transfiguration here is like that in the final scene of *Die Bürger von Calais* when the light illuminates the façade of the church to signal the triumphant apotheosis of Eustache de Saint-Pierre. But in *Gas II* it is only a moment; the Yellow Figures invade, the dome opening to the heavens is closed, the sun is shut out and replaced by the light of the arc-lamps. The final word of this act 'Gas' contrasts powerfully with the opening word of the act's first speech 'Morgen'.

The *Gas* trilogy demonstrates clearly Kaiser's profound scepticism about the possibility of ever freeing man from his enslavement by twentieth-century technology, capitalism and militarism. In its bitter irony it also suggests that the idealist may be even more dangerous to society than the technocrat and the demagogue. It is not the robot-like Blue and Yellow Figures or the Chief Engineer who destroy mankind but 'the chosen one' (F.P. 271) and he, the

Millionaire-Worker, destroys it out of despair and con-
tempt. Writes the critic Sokel: 'Beyond the Millionaire-
Worker's mystical quietism there emerges the goal of a
literal "quietism". The quiet of the grave descends upon a
world whose true salvation is annihilation.'[6]

'Das Floss der Medusa' ('The Raft of the Medusa')

Das Floss der Medusa was written between 1940 and 1943
when Kaiser was in exile in Switzerland; that such a prolific
writer took so long to write the play may have been due to
his lack of a permanent domicile, to the absence of his
family and friends who could provide intellectual stimula-
tion, and to his dire financial situation. The unusually long
gestation period may also be a result of Kaiser's having
radically altered his original concept as to how the central
incident of the play should be dramatised. That incident
concerned the sinking of a ship carrying refugee children
from the bombed cities of England to Canada in 1940,
when only a few of the children found safety in the
lifeboats. Kaiser wrote to Caesar von Arx in September
1940 outlining the play:

> There are only children in the lifeboat. The stage is the
> billowing sea with this unique boat. . . .
> A boy is the leading character. Maturing because of the
> experience, he directs the little group in the boat.
> A little child dies – he is released overboard and is
> solemnly lowered into the sea.
> Another boy imagines himself as Robinson, – until all
> realise they will never land again.
> Now only deep reflections on life and the parting from it.
> From the mouths of children. Moving.

159

Condemnation of the adults who commit such crimes: to let children drift in a boat on the open sea.
Into their certain death. But dawn comes. And with the rising day comes the seaplane.
The children are saved.
Only one does not let himself be saved: that boy. He does not want to return to this cursed life. He is disgusted by it. He grew up and says no. This is the great figure of the drama: a child who rejects us adults, spits at us – and rightfully so.
The boat capsizes, the boy drowns.[7]

It is clear from this scenario that Kaiser intended to present an idealised picture of childhood innocence as opposed to the corruption of the world of experience. But as he worked on the play he rejected this conventional approach to childhood: the children turn out to be as monstrous and corrupt as adults. On 17 January 1943 Kaiser wrote to von Arx:

Das Floss der Medusa progresses very slowly. Every crime committed by the adults is already traced out in these children. The ten-year olds cold-bloodedly murder the thirteenth child in the lifeboat – because Christianity is when more than twelve eat from the same meal. CAESAR. I have looked at humanity's naked navel – I will write down what I saw. That is my courage and my curse.[8]

Kaiser's letters reveal also that he was initially convinced that the play was unstageable because all the parts must be played by children, some of them very young, but after encouraging praise from friends, especially from Bernhard Diebold, he gradually became enthusiastic about the play, promoting it as a 'unique phenomenon in world literature'.

His attempts to have *Das Floss der Medusa* published were unsuccessful (it was first published in 1963), and several plans to stage it in Zürich were not executed due, in part, to his status as an exile which complicated matters. It finally received its premiere at the Basel Stadttheater on 24 February 1945 directed by Robert Pirk, a fellow German refugee and a long-time friend of Kaiser; the children who played the various roles were non-professional actors. The play was performed once more in Basel on 19 March and in Zürich on 21 April. The German premiere took place on 30 August 1948 in the Berlin Hebbel-Theater, with Reva Holsey as director; it was also produced in England in 1951 at the Watergate Theatre, London, in the translation by Koenigsgarten and Weisstein. None of the performances were particularly successful, partly because of the fact that the language – the language of adults and not of children – lacks the ecstasy and fervour of Kaiser's earlier Expressionist plays, and also because Kaiser (like Toller in his last play *Pastor Hall*) was too closely involved in his subject matter. Only three months before his death he writes to Caesar von Arx:

I am ALLAN – I described myself in him – I envy him for his early death. I had to live for so long and suffer every atrocity of life. I was not ALLAN in the boat – I became ALLAN on the rack of life.[9]

The play opens with a prologue in the form of stage directions meant to suggest the bombing and sinking of the ship; it is followed by a lament in the form of a *Mittelachsengedicht*, a poem in symmetrical form structured around an axis, in this case, the word MEDUSA. The play itself is divided into seven scenes each depicting one day in the lifeboat. The epilogue describing the protagonist's death is again a *Mittelachsengedicht*; this poem revolves around the words: WIE GEKREUZIGT (AS IF CRUCIFIED), and the last line of the poem (and of the play) echoes closely the final words of Christ on the cross: WIEDER EINMAL IST ES VOLLBRACHT (ONCE AGAIN IT IS CONSUMMATED).

The lifeboat contains thirteen children, only three of whom are named: the twelve-year-old Allan and Ann are the leaders of the group and they represent the protagonist and antagonist respectively; the mute nine-year-old Füchslein (Little Fox) becomes the victim of the struggle between Allan and Ann. Ann is a religious fanatic convinced that because they are thirteen they will be drowned:

> Jesus leads everyone into temptation, so that they will believe in him. That's why we are on this boat. The ship would have never been torpedoed if you'd felt more respect for Jesus and his twelve apostles – who make thirteen altogether. We've got you to thank that we're out here in the middle of the ocean now, all ready to sink if a storm comes up. And with thirteen here it will come up.[10]

Although Allan tries to neutralise Ann's fanaticism, he is no match for her. She persuades the children that one of them must die, the one who picks the ball with the black cross on it in a lottery. Allan discovers that Ann has drawn the ballot with the cross and, attracted by her vitality, he saves her by destroying all the lots. Still convinced that someone must be sacrificed Ann selects Füchslein as her victim. 'He won't feel a thing when we throw him into the water', she argues callously. 'I bet he'll quit breathing with his first swallow. He's just in the way here – and that's why it has to be him' (p. 31). To Allan's plea that they must act

162

like Christians she counters: 'Commandments are all right for the Sunday sermon and sound great in church. But outside it's very different: out here the greatest evil is thirteen' (p. 32).

Aware of Allan's feelings for her, Ann now tempts him to go through the ritual of a marriage service and when they retire to the little tent in the bow of the boat the other children, at Ann's instigation, throw Füchslein, whom Allan had protected until then, overboard. The following day a rescue plane, alerted by Ann's red thermos-bottle containing a message, arrives. Unaware of the children's crime the pilot attributes their devilish looks to their ordeal in the boat. Allan refuses to be rescued and to return to 'civilisation', because mankind is 'dead set on doing wrong, no matter where or why' and because 'children will be like grownups – because they are like them already!' (p. 49). Left alone in the lifeboat, Allan is killed in a strafing attack by an enemy plane which he attracted with Füchslein's flash-light.

Das Floss der Medusa marks a return after more than twenty years to Kaiser's Expressionist period; indeed there are striking parallels between his last play and *Die Bürger von Calais*, his first triumph in the Expressionist mode. Both include a lottery, in both the lottery is voided, in both the protagonists commit suicide. The plays differ in the vision which they embody. There is no figure so corrupt in *Die Bürger von Calais* as the twelve-year-old girl Ann; she is a demagogue, a Gorgon bringing death to everyone opposing her. She knows how to manipulate people, here the children, who represent the spineless and faceless masses without imagination and morality. They become Ann's willing accomplices because of the thrill the crime provides. After she has persuaded the children to murder Füchslein, the directions read: '*Ann's voice can no longer*

163

be heard from the fog. But there is one sound which can be heard ever louder and louder: it is the word "Yes" repeated excitedly and finally chanted in perfect unison. Then the drum is heard again – triumphant and wild' (p. 39). The chorus here echoes that of the Workers in the *Gas* plays as they cry out, 'Gas!' and 'Giftgas!'

The boy Allan is a strikingly tragic figure and Kaiser's letters testify to his particularly close identification with him. In April 1943 he wrote to his friend, Julius Marx: 'In Allan I have depicted myself and poured out the disillusionment which I have experienced in life. I came into this life with the purest perceptions and have been completely soiled by it. Besides disdain I know only pain . . .'[11] Allan is a Christ-like protagonist, a Eustache de Saint-Pierre driven to death by an existential despair. His white scarf which he turns into a sail is blown away by the wind – his message remains unheard – while the red thermos-bottle belonging to Ann is found and restores the children to an existence which is irredeemably corrupt. Clearly Ann, figure of the anti-Christ, triumphs over the Christ-like Allan, who dying 'lies with arms outstretched upon the center bench: As if crucified' (p. 50).

In contrast to Toller, who never completely lost his belief in the possible regeneration of man (the church bells at the close of *Pastor Hall* sound a message of hope throughout the world), Kaiser rejects the possibility of regeneration in the *Gas* trilogy and in this play. The rejection is all the more significant in that the final vision of evil is personified in children. But haunting much of Kaiser's work is the figure of Christ, archetype of crucified mankind. The outline of Kaiser's uncompleted novel *Ard*, scribbled on an envelope virtually minutes before he died, ends with Jesus hanging on the cross beside Ard, saviour and sinner linked through their tragic participation in existence. This final scene is of a

piece with Kaiser's *oeuvre* and of a piece with the final
scene of *Das Floss der Medusa*:

> And on this sea of blood the boat drifts on,
> Half sunk, because its sides are full of bullet-holes.
> Allan lies with arms outstretched upon the centre bench:
> > As if crucified
> The water rushes in and laps at Allan's body.
> > The boat sinks deeper.
> A sudden wave rushes over it,
> And when the wave recedes, the boat has disappeared.
> And once more the crime is consummated.

Notes and References

1. Expressionism

1. K. Edschmid, 'Expressionismus in der Dichtung', *Deutsche Literaturkritik im zwanzigsten Jahrhundert*, ed. H. Mayer (Stuttgart: Henry Goverts Verlag, 1965) p. 265.

2. M. Hamburger and C. Middleton (eds and trans), *Modern German Poetry* (New York: Grove Press, 1962) p. 48.

3. K. Pinthus (ed.), *Menschheitsdämmerung* (Hamburg: Rowohlt, 1959) pp. 25, 28.

4. See A. Arnold, *Die Literatur des Expressionismus* (Stuttgart: Kohlhammer, 1966) pp. 22–3.

5. H. Marx, 'August Stramm', *The Drama Review*, 19, no. 3, September 1975, 17.

6. Hamburger and Middleton, *Modern German Poetry*, p. 22.

7. M. Gordon, 'German Expressionist Acting', *The Drama Review*, 19, No. 3, 1975, 42.

8. N. Hern, 'Expressionism', *The German Theatre*, ed. R. Hayman (London: Oswald Wolff, 1975) p. 116.

9. K. Macgowan and R. E. Jones, *Continental Stagecraft* (New York: Benjamin Blom, 1922) pp. 130–1.

10. Pinthus, *Menschheitsdämmerung*, p. 12.

Notes and References

2. Ernst Toller: Art and Politics

1. The play was first published in German in *Ernst Toller. Gesammelte Werke*, eds J. M. Spalek and W. Frühwald (Munich: Carl Hanser, 1978) Vol. 3.

3. The New Man: Birth and Crucifixion

1. M. Patterson, *The Revolution in German Theatre, 1900–1933* (London: Routledge & Kegan Paul, 1981) p. 102.
2. Quoted in T. Bütow, *Der Konflikt zwischen Revolution und Pazifismus im Werk Ernst Tollers* (Hamburg: Hartmut Lüdke, 1975) p. 84.
3. H. Jhering, *Von Reinhardt bis Brecht* (Reinbek: Rowohlt, 1967) p. 53.
4. In 1959 Kortner still remembers the premiere: 'The press – especially Kerr – was extraordinary. After the success of this evening I ceased worrying about my career. The theatres were wooing me eagerly' (T. 6/100).
5. M. Gordon, 'German Expressionist Acting', *The Drama Review*, 19, no. 3, 1975, 38, 46.
6. M. Patterson, *The Revolution in German Theatre, 1900–1933*, p. 100.
7. Sarah Sonja Lerch, the wife of a university lecturer, was a leader of the striking ammunition workers in Munich, 1918. She was arrested together with Toller and other strike leaders in February 1918.
8. Piscator had also planned a production of *Die Wandlung* at his theatre, Das Tribunal, in Königsberg in the winter of 1919/20 'which was to differ in principle from the Berlin [Karl Heinz Martin] production in that the settings were to be constructed as realistically as possible (the reality of the war as I had actually experienced it)'. E. Piscator, *The Political Theatre*, trans. H. Rorrison (London: Eyre Methuen, 1980) pp. 22–3. Piscator also wanted a more 'realistic' style in *Die Wandlung*: 'I even reworked the language in order to suggest to Toller (may he forgive me, the blackness of this thought is unknown to him to this day!) how he might free his style of its lyrical Expressionism. The Expressionist School provided no pointer for me.' Ibid., p. 23.
9. Macgowan and Jones, *Continental Stagecraft*, p. 148.
10. Ibid., p. 152.
11. M. Patterson, *The Revolution in German Theatre, 1900–1933*, p. 115.

4. Man versus Society

1. Patterson quotes P. Wiecke as being the director of the 1923 premiere in Leipzig but it was A. Kronacher. Wiecke directed the play in the 1924 Dresden production.

2. J. M. Spalek, *Ernst Toller and his Critics, A Bibliography* (Charlottesville, Va.: The University Press, 1968) p. 589.

3. Toller changed this ending in the 1924 edition, where Hinkemann does not die. Left alone he delivers a final speech:

> She was strong and sound. And she broke the net. And here I stand – monstrous – ridiculous. In all ages there'll be men like me. But why me? Why should it fall on me? It doesn't pick and choose. It hits this man and that man. And the next and the next go free. What can we know about it? Where from? Where to? Any day the kingdom of heaven may arise, any night the great flood may come and swallow up the earth. (S.P. 193)

4. Toller chose the names for many of his protagonists in order to underline their characteristic features. Hinkemann's first name Eugen, meaning the well-born, emphasises the discrepancy between Hinkemann's apparent good health and his sexual impotence.

5. Piscator, *Political Theatre*, p. 335.

6. J. Willett, *The Theatre of Erwin Piscator* (London: Eyre Methuen, 1978) p. 117.

7. M. Patterson, *The Revolution in German Theatre, 1900–1933*, p. 123.

8. Piscator, *Political Theatre*, p. 207.

9. Willett, *Erwin Piscator*, p. 84.

10. M. Patterson, *The Revolution in German Theatre, 1900–1933*, p. 139.

11. Ibid., p. 145.

12. C. D. Innes, *Erwin Piscator's Political Theatre* (Cambridge: The University Press, 1972) p. 100.

13. Ibid., p. 158.

14. Piscator, *Political Theatre*, p. 216.

15. The play was first published in English. It was first published in German in vol. 3 of the Frühwald/Spalek edition. In one of the earlier versions Toller has Pastor Hall die of a heart attack. T. Engel used this version in his 1947 Berlin production.

16. *Pastor Hall* (English version) p. 19.

17. Ibid., p. 52.

18. Ibid., pp. 72, 73–4.

19. Ibid., p. 79.

5. Georg Kaiser: Life and Art

1. Quoted in G. M. Valk, 'Georg Kaiser: Ansätze zu einer Biographie', *Georg Kaiser*, ed. A. Arnold (Stuttgart: Ernst Klett, 1980) p. 8.
2. Ibid., pp. 10–11.
3. *Georg Kaiser, Briefe*, ed. G. M. Valk (Frankfurt: Propyläen Verlag, 1980) p. 180.
4. Ibid., p. 879.
5. Valk, 'Georg Kaiser', *Georg Kaiser*, p. 18.
6. Valk, *Briefe*, p. 248.
7. Ibid., p. 483.

6. The New Man: Apotheosis and Decline

1. M. Patterson, *The Revolution in German Theatre, 1900–1933*, p. 62.
2. A. Arnold, *Die Literatur des Expressionismus*, p. 119.
3. N. Frye, *Anatomy of Criticism* (Princeton, NJ: Princeton University Press, 1957) p. 286.
4. Brecht's short story 'Der verwundete Sokrates' ('The Wounded Sokrates') is based on the play and dedicated to Kaiser. Despite his fascination with *Der gerettete Alkibiades* Brecht criticised its 'unnecessary' length. In his story he wanted to demonstrate how and where Kaiser should have ended his play.
5. Valk, *Briefe*, pp. 174–5.
6. I retain the German spelling when I discuss Kaiser's recreation of Socrates and Alcibiades.
7. *Alkibiades Saved*, trans. B. Q. Morgan, in *An Anthology of German Drama*, ed. W. H. Sokel (New York: Doubleday, 1963) pp. 219–20. (Future page references in the text are to this edition.)

7. Technology and Armageddon

1. See E. Schürer, 'Die *Gas* Dramen', in Arnold, *Georg Kaiser*, pp. 92–3.
2. Valk, *Briefe*, p. 159.
3. Ibid., p. 136.
4. B. Diebold, *Der Denkspieler Georg Kaiser* (Frankfurt/M.: Frankfurter Verlagsanstalt, 1929) p. 76.
5. M. Patterson, *The Revolution in German Theatre, 1900–1933*, p. 46.

6. W. H. Sokel, *The Writer in Extremis: Expressionism in Twentieth-Century German Literature* (Stanford, Cal.: The University Press, 1959) p. 202.

7. Valk, *Briefe*, p. 556.

8. Ibid., p. 828.

9. Ibid., p. 1110.

10. *The Raft of the Medusa*, trans. G. E. Wellwarth, *Postwar German Theatre*, eds and trans M. Benedikt and G. E. Wellwarth (New York: E. P. Dutton, 1967) p. 17. (Future page references in the text are to this edition.)

11. Valk, *Briefe*, p. 869.

Selected Bibliography

(i) Primary Sources

Benedikt, M. and G. E. Wellwarth (eds and trans), *Postwar German Theatre, An Anthology of Plays* (New York: E. P. Dutton, 1967).

Huder, Walther (ed.), *Georg Kaiser, Werke* (Frankfurt/M.: Propyläen Verlag, 1970–72), 6 volumes.

Kenworthy, B. J., R. Last and J. M. Ritchie (trans), *Five Plays, Georg Kaiser* (London: Calder and Boyars, 1971).

Sokel, Walter H. (ed.), *An Anthology of German Expressionist Drama* (New York: Doubleday, 1963).

Spalek, John and Wolfgang Frühwald (eds), *Ernst Toller, Gesammelte Werke/Kommentar und Materialien* (Munich: Carl Hanser, 1978–9), 6 volumes.

Spender, Stephen and Hugh Hunt (trans), *Pastor Hall by Ernst Toller* (New York: Random House, 1939).

Toller, Ernst, Hermann Kesten, Mary Baker Eddy (eds), *Seven Plays by Ernst Toller* (London: The Bodley Head, 1935).

Valk, Gesa M. (ed.), *Georg Kaiser, Briefe* (Frankfurt/M.: Propyläen Verlag, 1980).

(ii) Secondary Sources

Arnold, Armin (ed.), *Georg Kaiser* (Stuttgart: Ernst Klett, 1980).

Bablet, Denis and Jean Jacquot (eds), *L'Expressionisme dans le Théâtre*

171

Européen (Paris: Editions du Centre National de la Recherche Scientifique, 1971).

Diebold, Bernhard, *Anarchie im Drama* (Frankfurt/M.: Frankfurter Verlagsanstalt, 1921).

Diebold, Bernhard, *Der Denkspieler Georg Kaiser* (Frankfurt/M.: Frankfurter Verlagsanstalt, 1929).

Hern, Nicholas, 'Expressionism', *The German Theatre* (ed.), R. Hayman (London: Wolff, 1975).

Kenworthy, B. J., *Georg Kaiser* (Oxford: Basil Blackwell, 1957).

Knellessen, F. W., *Agitation auf der Bühne: Das politische Theater der Weimarer Republik* (Emsdetten: Lechte Verlag, 1970).

Macgowan, Kenneth and R. E. Jones, *Continental Stagecraft* (New York: Harcourt, Brace, 1922).

Ossar, Michael, *Anarchism in The Dramas of Ernst Toller* (Albany: State University of New York Press, 1980).

Patterson, Michael, *The Revolution in German Theatre, 1900–1933* (London: Routledge & Kegan Paul, 1981).

Pausch, Holger A. and Ernest Reinhold (eds), *Georg Kaiser Symposium* (Berlin: Agora Verlag, 1980).

Piscator, Erwin, *The Political Theatre*, trans. H. Rorrison (London: Eyre Methuen, 1980).

Ritchie, J. M., *German Expressionist Drama* (Boston: Twayne, 1976).

Schürer, Ernst, *Georg Kaiser* (New York: Twayne, 1971).

Sokel, Walter H., *The Writer in Extremis: Expressionism in Twentieth-Century German Literature* (Stanford, Cal.: The University Press, 1959).

Willett, John, *The Theatre of Erwin Piscator* (London: Methuen, 1978).

Index

Index

Index

Index

Index